Jazz Danceology

Teaching and Choreographing Jazz Dance

By: Marcus R. Alford with Marsha Proser Cohen

Foreword by: Joseph H. Mazo
Introduction by: Gus Giordano

Published by Dance Press
Marietta, Georgia

ACKNOWLEDGEMENTS

My thanks to the following for their love and contributions to the ART of JAZZ DANCE...

Alvin Ailey
Phoebe Barr
Judy Ann Bassing
Douglas Bentz
Pepsi Bethel
Tatina Bezuglaya
Sergie Bezugly
Jack Cole
Keith Anthony R. Cross
Vic D'Amore
Dance Educators of America
Dance Masters of America
Dance Teachers Club of Boston, Inc.
Lea Darwin
Annie Day
Ronnie DeMarco
Mercedes Ellington
Bob Fosse
Jana Frances-Fischer
Joseph Giacobbe
Gus Giordano
Sherry Gold
Lynette Grubb (for opening my eyes and heart to the art of Tap Dance)
Frank Hatchett
Ginny East Hendry
Cathy Lee Hess
Robert Ivey
Charles Kelly
Meribeth Kisner
Dagmar Kossman
Herb Kossover
T. Meriah Kruse
Luigi
Matt Mattox
Joseph H. Mazo
Jeff Mildenstein
Duncan Noble
Pattie Obey
Papa Jazz Record Shoppe, Columbia, SC
Amparo Olmedo
Peter Powlus
Bebe Quail
Gunther Rebel
Petra Schulte-Kölpin
Vickie Sheer
Billy Siegenfield
Bill Spencer
Delia Stewart
Art Stone
Tommy Sutton (the "soulman" of Tap Dance)
Fred Traguth
Joe Tremaine
Julie Walder
Lou Wall (for beginning it all)
Dan Youmans
The Members of *the JAZZ ON TAP* Dance Festival
The members of the "hot and sassy" *JAZZ DANCE THEATRE SOUTH*

Photography by: Denny Cohen, Marden Photographers

Design collaboration by: Pam McClure, McClure Publishing

Models: Marcus Alford, Annie Day, Bridget Guenthner, Dawn Guthrie, Sharon Wilson Jacobs, Emily King, Michael Perez, Jodi Wagers, Arprentis Weems

Copyright © 1991 by Dance Press, a subsidiary of Marden, Inc.
All rights reserved including the right of reproduction in whole or in part in any form.

Published by Dance Press
147 Powers Ferry Road
Marietta, Georgia 30067

ISBN: 1-880716-00-3

For

Annie and Devin
Rachel and Josh

With love,
Marcus and Marsha

DEDICATION

Jazz, it has been stated, is the dance of the 20th century. It is the most popular class for older students and the goal to which younger ones aspire. Yet, it is new. To date, there are only a few books that even refer to jazz dancing and still fewer that attempt to explain or teach it.

There is an urgent need for a text on technique and style of this rapidly growing art form. Because jazz is so new, a great percentage of dance teachers have had little or no real training in jazz. The regional, national, and international workshops are ever increasing and constantly working to address jazz in the curriculum. Thousands of dance professionals are unable to attend regularly and many who do, agree that there must be additional learning tools. They recognize the need for a text in jazz. They believe that they must be able to meet the demands of their students or risk losing them to someone who can.

In *Jazz Danceology*, I have attempted to fulfill that need. I have included history, terminology and explanations of techniques and exercises. Several classes, each with a detailed curriculum and lesson plan, have been outlined for you along with methodology and accompanying music. Photos have been added for further explanation and demonstration.

Music is listed by instrument as well as type to enable you to select the appropriate music for class exercise and performance. There is also a section with choreography to get you started. I've also left lots of space throughout for your own notes.

This book was written as an aid to teaching jazz. I dedicate *Jazz Danceology* to you, the dance professionals throughout the world, who, through your dedication and love of dance, will ensure that jazz, the dance of the 20th century, will continue as a vital art form into the 21st century and beyond.

Marcus

FOREWORD
by Joseph H. Mazo

Ballet is the dominant theatrical dance form of Western culture partly because within that culture it is universal. Members of Dance Theater of Harlem appear as guest artists with the Royal Ballet in London; performers from Copenhagen are comfortably at home when taking class in New York. Four hundred years of experiment and development have produced a movement vocabulary shared by ballet dancers throughout the world. That does not mean that the art is static. Succeeding generations have altered and augmented the original intent and technique so thoroughly that Louis XIV would not recognize Balanchine's "Agon" as ballet; 'Leaps? Lifts? Ladies dancing on their toes? Ma foi! C'es magnifique, mais c'est n'est pas la danse.' Whenever stagnation began to set in, some genius—Petipa, Fokine, Balanchine—introduced a stream of fresh ideas, yet the basic code of steps has been maintained.

Jazz is far younger than ballet, so young, indeed, that it is still defining and expanding the territory it inhabits. This book, addressed primarily to teachers, is an attempt to set some markers. Marcus Alford seeks to establish an agreed upon vocabulary — kinetic and linguistic — that instructors can use in working with students. He does not propose this as a restriction on creativity, but as a starting place for it. He understands that jazz, like other arts, needs an accepted, common language and a systematic syllabus in order to develop its full potential.

The potential for jazz, I think, is greater than generally is realized. Jazz often has been treated with less respect than it deserves because it is not regarded as a "serious" art form. There are several reasons for this. For one thing, jazz (music and dance) is associated with popular entertainment. People seem to believe that art, like medicine, cannot be effective if it is enjoyable. Second, jazz comes out of vernacular dancing. It sometimes is assumed that the general populace cannot possibly be trusted to produce art. Third, and perhaps most important, jazz did not originate in the dominant stratum of American culture. It was created by the descendants of slaves. Less than 50 years ago, popular wisdom still insisted that blacks 'had a natural sense of rhythm' meaning, of course, that they did not really work at music or dance, and that their creations were not art but merely manifestations of genetics.

All of these beliefs leads to the erroneous conviction that jazz is simple. In fact, listening to jazz (and dancing to it) is as demanding as listening to the music we call classical, by which we mean "serious." It might be well to remember that during his lifetime, Verdi, who gave us the magnificent music of *Aida* and *La Traviata*, to name two, was not "classical," but was the most popular composer in Italy.

Jazz will be regarded as a serious art when we have learned to take it seriously. Teaching jazz is as demanding as teaching ballet or modern dance. It requires an intense dedication and a strong insistence on safety, technique, discipline, and creativity. This book assumes that jazz dance is a serious, complex, potentially unlimited art that can be studied, analyzed, and taught. It suggests that teachers think of jazz not as a series of formulas or routines, but as a form of expression that, like all such forms, requires a vocabulary, a technique, and sense of purpose.

TABLE OF CONTENTS

Acknowledgements	2
Dedication	4
Foreword by Joseph H. Mazo	5
Introduction by Gus Giordano	8

CHAPTER 1
History of Jazz Dancing	9
Thoughts on Jazz from Some of the Greats	12

CHAPTER 2
What is Jazz Dance?	35
Styles of Jazz	37

CHAPTER 3
Placement, Plumb Line Theory	44
Terminolgy and Technique	46
Preparations	
Jumps, Leaps, and Hops	103
Turns	110
PBS Theory	111

CHAPTER 4
Planning a Jazz Class	119
Exercise: Standing to Floor to Standing	120
Class #1 - Begin Standing	125
Partner Stretches	127
Class #2 - Begin on Floor	132
Minimum Age for Jazz Students	133
Beginners Jazz Class	134
Intermediate Jazz Class	135
Advanced Jazz Class	136
Children's Jazz Class	137
Teen Jazz Class	137
Adult Jazz Class	137

CHAPTER 5
Tips for Successful Choreography	139
Staging	140
Diagrams for Classroom and Stage	141
Abbreviations for Terminology and Techniques	145
Routines:	
Red Hot Chicago	147
Everybody Dance	149
Dr. Feelgood	152
War Dance	154
Trance Dance	157
More	159
Sooner or Later	162
Fever	164

CHAPTER 6
Music	
Origins of Word "Jazz"	167
Classical Jazz	169
Big Bands and Composers	171
Blues	173
Jazz Rock Fusion	174
New Age	176
Contemporary/Current Jazz	177

CONCLUSION
	179

APPENDIX
Dictionary of Often Used Ballet Terms	181
Abbreviations for Terminology and Techniques	183
Bibliography	185
Index	186

INTRODUCTION
By Gus Giordano
Founder/Director: American Jazz Dance World Congress

Because of jazz's accessibility to the mass audience, it has usually been regarded as a dance for peasants and is therefore, continually overlooked by critics and balletomanes. If jazz dance is accepted, it is only when it is presented as an historical art form, especially when depicting the mood of the 30's, 40's, or 50's. The acceptance of jazz dance has been categorized as the music and dance of TV. It is regarded as artificial in nature and choreographed by technicians or the TV videographers. The dancers subsequently become clones of the featured "Top 40" singer of the moment. Through the years, it has become further and further from the feeling and soul of jazz.

When I became acquainted with jazz dance in the 50's, it was called modern jazz dance, partly because it was the dance of the time but also because often modern dance was used as the basic teaching structure. We had no complete body warm-up specifically devoted to jazz dance. Some early teachers used African movements or a ballet warm up. Some used the isolation exercises of Indian dance or the swinging rhythms of tap dance. Since those formative days, jazz dance has produced more sophisticated methods for teaching the strength, flexibility, and power control the total jazz dancer requires.

We cannot ignore the progress made in jazz, but nor can we, as teachers and serious students of this unique American dance form, lose sight of the principles and discipline of dance: the training of the total dancer.

It is with great pride that I endorse this book as a valuable contribution to this never ending effort of jazz teachers and students to establish our rightful place in the world of dance.

Photo: Camera Room

CHAPTER 1

THAT ELECTRIC, ECLECTIC DANCE CALLED "JAZZ"

A HISTORY OF JAZZ DANCING by Jana E. Frances-Fischer

What is jazz dance? Where did it come from? There are no simple answers to these questions. The term jazz dance means different things to different people. Teachers, choreographers, historians, and performers hold individual views about how this art form developed and came into its own. Without a doubt, one fact is certain: jazz dance is a dynamic, ever- changing dance genre, always open to snapping up new movement ideas and soaking up the latest cultural styles. Jazz dance is hot, cool, sassy, smooth, sharp, high, low, big, delicate. Jazz is an important subject matter in any dance curriculum. Jazz dance is a wonderful form of exercise, stimulating mind and body alike. Jazz is an exciting art form to watch, to create, to be a part of.

Yet, the origin of the word "jazz" still remains an unsolved mystery. Jazz could have come from the jass or razz bands from the Southern U.S., particularly New Orleans, at the turn of the century. The style they played was called "Ragtime," "Blues," or "Dixieland." This music was mainly the domain of black artists. These musical forms, incorporating syncopation, European harmonies, complex rhythms of West Africa, and American gospel singing, were to become known as "jazz." This sound naturally inspired movement, and "jazz dance" was born.

Speculation about these two American art forms, jazz music and jazz dance, is that their influences sparked one another. They evolved sometimes together and other times separately. The roots of jazz dance borrow from a melting pot: a mixture of world cultural traditions. Jazz dance, as we know it today, is a blend of two main movement ideas: folk dances from Africa, North and South America, and Europe, and theater dance evolving from modern, ballet, and ethnic dance.

In the early 1900's, concert staples were tap, soft shoe, and ballroom dances. These steps were often the cornerstones of minstrel shows and vaudeville acts. Also during this era, over one hundred zippy, fast-paced popular dances came and went in America. By the Flapper era of the 1920's, Dixieland music, with its fast Ragtime beat, spread from New Orleans up the Mississippi and on to Chicago and New York. This music generated energetic dancing, equally as vigorous. Famous dances of this period included the Charleston, the Shimmy, and the Lindy hop. Catchy rhythms and fun steps served to sway popular opinion in favor of these styles of dance. Bill "Bojangles" Robinson, an important black tap dancer of the day, elevated the rhythmic structure, precise footwork, and complexity of steps to professional standards during the 1920's.

Into the 1930's spotlight came the legendary Jitterbug as well as several Latin influenced dances such as the Rhumba and the Conga. Fred Astaire and Ginger Rogers, a dynamic dancing duo, combined balletic elegance and jazzy percussive accents to sustain a long and fruitful partnership on stage and screen. Their per- formances created an acceptance for what would evolve into jazz dance.

The Swing era of the 1940's marked a major dance boom, accelerated by frequent nationwide radio broadcasts. Movies, ballroom dancing, musical theater, and nightclub performances also helped increase the great appeal of jazz dance and jazz music. The broadway musical, *Oklahoma!*, choreographed by Agnes De Mille, was the first overt attempt in musical theater history to advance the story line by using jazz-like choreography.

Also, the forties witnessed the development of jazz dance into a serious dance form. Specialized techniques and choreographic styles were budding at studios and in some colleges. Key individuals of this important time with their own unique styles included Jack Cole, often considered the "father" of jazz dance. Cole trained in modern and Asian dance forms. This combination proved successful for nightclub, musical and film choreography. Katherine Dunham and Pearl Primus were both fascinated by the ethnic origins of jazz dance. Their philosophies of teaching and choreography were grounded in Afro-Haitian and West Indies traditions.

In the mid-1950's, ballet and modern dance sprouted their wings in the U.S. and their widespread appeal helped push jazz dance into a new growth spurt. Plays, musicals, movies and television exposed jazz dance in a new light and helped to legitimize it as a performing art not merely as an entertainment. In 1957, noted choreographer Jerome Robbins used jazz movement, rooted in ballet, to depict volatile street-gang life in New York City in the widely acclaimed, highly "dancy" musical, *West Side Story*. This is viewed by many theorists and artists as the true beginning of jazz dance as we know it today. A new talent, Matt Mattox (a Cole dancer), became identified with a linear, percussive style which he incorporated into his Broadway, concert dance, and television choreography.

In the 1960's, Gus Giordano (modern-based technique), Luigi (ballet oriented), and other giants of jazz began to carve their own niches and the face of jazz dance changed from "fun" to the realm of the highly skilled dancer. During this decade, the identifiable styles and techniques of the jazz greats emerged.

In the 1970's, Bob Fosse (*Chicago, Dancin', All That Jazz*) and Michael Bennett (*Chorus Line, Dream Girls*) created a series of exciting dance-oriented musicals and films where the choreography is slick, sensual, fast-paced and highly charged.

The decade of the 1980's introduced "hot jazz" in music videos, concerts, TV shows, movies, plays, and musicals. At this time, experimentation with a myriad of street dance forms, "popping", "locking", and "break dancing" could be seen on the street corner. Their influence carried over into music videos, movies and even concert dance.

Jazz dance is America's unique, multi-cultural contribution to the world of dance. Jazz expresses certain feelings, emotions, and attitudes about the world we live in and communicates them in a direct style, distinctive from other forms of dance. Jazz dance is the vocabulary and the subject matter of American life. Its pulse reflects the diverse voice that makes up American culture. Therefore, jazz dance is constantly in a state of growth and change as it continues to mirror contemporary society. It moves with the tide and willingly incorporates new challenges in music, movement, and thought. Jazz dance traditions will continue to thrive, branch out, and take risks as jazz teachers, choreographers, students, and enthusiasts everywhere perpetuate this powerful art form and pass it on to the coming generations with dedication and fervor.

BIBLIOGRAPHY

Andreu, Helene. *Jazz Dance: An Adult Beginner's Guide.* New Jersey: Prentice-Hall, 1983.

Czompo, Ann. *Recreational Jazz Dance: A Syllabus of Jazz Dance Terms.* New York: State College of New York at Courtland, 1971.

Kennedy, Michael. *The Concise Oxford Dictionary of Music,* 3rd edition. England: Oxford University Press, 1980.

Kraines, Minda Goodman and Kan, Esther. *Jump Into Jazz,* 2nd edition. California: Mayfield Publishing Company, 1990.

Stearns, Marshall and Stearns, Jean. *Jazz Dance: The Story of American Vernacular Dance.* New York: MacMillan Publishers, 1968.

Photo: Mike Canale

Thoughts On Jazz From Some of the Greats...

What we learn from study and training increases our knowledge. What we learn from others builds on that knowledge and lends a different perspective to our teaching, choreographing and performing.

These dance professionals have generously offered the following contributions to *Jazz Danceology* to enable a broader base for understanding of jazz.

"I often wonder and look forward for the day to come when jazz dance speaks for itself, in its own voice without the benefit of mixing it up and commercialization."

Pepsi Bethel
Teacher, Choreographer
New York

"Jazz dance to me is truly the JOY of total freedom of expression and movement."

Judy Ann Bassing
International Teacher and Choreographer

"Within our programs and concerts we always include jazz works...to widen our range of appeal to the audience. Because we are competitive Ballroom dancers and must adhere to rules, we feel that Jazz Dance allows us the freedom to express our emotions."

**Sergie Bezugly and
Tatina Bezuglaya**
*Choreographers, Dancers, Teachers
and Chairman of the
Modern Dancing Club, "Extrond"
Smolensk, USSR*

" I think the essence of jazz music is personal style and expression. It has been said that a person should be able to recognize a jazz musician in just 3 or 4 bars. So strong and individual is his statement that it reveals exactly who he is as a person and what he feels about it as an artist. Jazz music by definition is personal and spontaneous.

"In the same way, jazz dancing and jazz dance training needs to concern itself with these issues. Rather than just drilling and rehashing the same old steps and vocabulary, and running about frantically learning all the 'latest 'steps on the latest video, we need to encourage our jazz dance students and artists to discover their own way of moving, their own style and voice, to express themselves as people and as artists so that in only 3 or 4 movements, we as an audience will know something about the dancer and how he feels about being alive. That's jazz! Don't just copy...create and express what you have to say, and most importantly, in your own style.

"Anything other than that is just like stuffing your soul in someone else's shoes. And man, that ain't jazz!"

Douglas Bentz
*Teacher, Choreographer
Point Park College, Pittsburgh, PA*

"Great dancing is a blur of good training in all elements of dance. Together Ballet, Modern and Jazz dance training have helped me to create a new and fresh way of utilizing choreography....it will be imperative that a dancer have had the broad training in which the quality and level of dancing is endless.!"

Keith Anthony R. Cross
Dancer, Teacher, Choreographer
Houston, Texas

"Want to dance Jazz? STUDY !!!... Jazz Dance is a fusion of many types of dance and countless styles of movement. Dance has been defined as a living and constantly changing art form. This being true then Jazz Dance is the quintessential form of dance being both vitally alive and always in a state of flux.

"Without getting into the myriad of Jazz Dance styles...suffice it to say the range is boundless and continual. On one end will be a style which is almost pure Ballet and on the other will be a style which will have little to no form. In between will be all the styles derived from culture and environment. This is the forging of all the tradition of ethnicity and all the reaction to our surroundings. Add to this the personal tastes in the music and/or sounds with which we dance, and the brew is a delicious potpourri called Jazz Dance....study different styles but always study the root - ballet."

Vic D'Amore
Teacher, Choreographer, Studio of Dance, Ltd.
New York

"I have always liked working in the jazz dance medium because it gave me vast and unlimited possibilities. Jazz dance is not a basic dance technique. It needs the fundamentals of ballet and modern dance to build upon and from there develops stylistically. Like the America from which it sprang, jazz dance is complex and contradictory...it thrives, passing through fad after fad and adapts itself to an amazing variety of conditions...like jazz music, it is perhaps the soul of American movement."

Lea Darwin
Dancer, Teacher, Choreographer
Florida

"Jazz Dance has something for everyone! It offers the student upbeat and challenging study, the performer an outlet for expression of style and technique, and the audience 100% entertainment."

Annie Day
Dancer, Teacher, Choreographer
Marietta, GA

"Jazz in dance as in music must have a strong base in order to create with knowledge of the instrument, the free individual interpretation of the form. You must know form to go off on form."

Mercedes Ellington,
Choreographer, Jazz and Tap Dance
Master Teacher, Director: Dance Ellington
New York

"A student's worst enemy is self judgments...when a child first learns to walk, that child is not concerned with whether the movement is correct or incorrect, whether or not it looks right. Its only concern is to walk. To learn, our minds must be like those of children, free of self imposed judgments, free to discover balance and progress on our own...students must be concerned with observing and feeling where the body is. To feel is to know.!"

Ronnie DeMarco
Dancer, Teacher, Choreographer
New York/Florida

"Jazz - a word that immediately brings to mind something essentially American, something appealing, something associated with the mainstream of our culture - a part of what is popular. It is difficult to categorize and doesn't fit comfortably into a simple mold or formula. It evokes contrasts: it's hot, yet it's cool; it's sophisticated and urbane, yet it can be low down; it can be rousing, or it can be blusey; it can be loud, or it can be quietly contained. But whatever it means at different times to different people, it is a form that is sensual and touches the feelings and emotions.

"Jazz Dance is certainly unique. For jazz dance to continue to acquire the credibility and artistic acceptance it seeks, it must push past its perceived image by some as merely cabaret, commercial, or show dancing. Not that there is anything less important about these genres, but many jazz champions want more for the image of jazz dance."

Joseph Giacobbe
Teacher, Choreographer
Metairie, LA

"Jazz Dancing is the soul of all people and touches everyone."

Gus Giordano,
Choreographer, Master Jazz Dance Teacher
Director: American Jazz Dance World Congress
Director: World Congress of Jazz Dance
Chicago, IL

Thoughts on Jazz / 18

"This book is certainly a welcomed and much needed addition to dance education today. In workshops as well as in my own studios, I have seen a tremendous upsurge in the demand for jazz dance classes. Though jazz may be based in ballet or modern with similarities to tap styles, knowledge of those art forms does not guarantee knowledge of jazz dance.

I am delighted to see a text on how to teach, perform and choreograph jazz. With the growing popularity of jazz dance, this book is a must for teachers and serious students of dance."

Lynette Grubb
*Teacher, Choreographer, Director: Dance Stop Company
Marietta, GA*

"Without technique you cannot last for any length of time. All should study every style, old and new. Jazz dance is boundless, a never ending newness."

Sherry Gold
*Choreographer, Master Teacher
Boston, MA*

Photo: Mike Canale

"I find that technique training in the jazz class is important because it gives jazz a connection, fusion and control to dance jazz properly."

Frank Hatchett
Choreographer, Jazz Dance Master Teacher
New York

Photo: Hendry

"Jazz is a form of dance which changes and evolves with each decade, carrying with it the trends and styles that are popular in fashion. To become a jazz dancer is a responsibility...A great jazz dancer can accept what is new and innovative, yet is also a stylist who has learned from the many artists who came before him. It requires devotion to technique, history and personal style to become a powerful jazz dancer. Technique enables us to control our bodies in the variety of ways necessary to be expressive. History gives us the material in which to build authentic dance which can depict a time frame or mood to our audience. Personal style is what sets us apart from others, creating a true jazz artist."

Ginny East Hendry
Teacher, Choreographer
Sarasota, FL

Photo: Bama Fine Arts Photography

"Jazz dance is universal. My experience has been that everyone finds some one thing or more to enjoy or relate to in jazz dance. By its very essence, it is a common language, reaching deep inside and drawing upon the very soul of us all."

Cathy Lee Hess
Director of Dance, Carver Creative Arts Magnet High School
Montgomery, AL

"Technique quickly delineates the 'fad' dancer from the truly trained 'jazz' dancer. A good solid technique utilizes the skills and background of good basic ballet and are well defined in the body lines and control seen in the American jazz dance artist."

Robert Ivey
Choreographer, Artistic Director: Robert Ivey Ballet
Charleston, SC

"Jazz Dance today has many facets...but this book of jazz dance history and terminology will insure that the technical aspect of jazz dance is not lost."

Charles Kelly
Teacher, Choreographer
New York

Thoughts on Jazz / 22

Photo: Ron Pomerantz

"I am delighted at the response of American audiences to jazz. The response is full of energy and delight, but I continue to be amazed that it still has a 'shady' reputation in the art circles. It seems to be valued less than Ballet or Modern and yet, it is so accepted by its audiences....jazz is high energy—jazz has a sensuality about it. Some of these qualities seem to be its 'undoing' in art circles. I suggest that as it has grown and matured from its birth, it has evolved into its own personality. This personality reflects the moods, trends, styles, politics, religious beliefs of American people. Hopefully all will accept this 'art' form in its own right...I am excited about the future of American Jazz Dance not only in America but on a global scale....the possibilities are endless and exciting."

Meribeth Kisner
Dancer, Teacher, Choreographer
Director: Chi-Town Jazz Dance Co.
Evanston, IL

Photo: Heike Wippermann

"Taking (jazz) from American Jazz teachers, I've learned faster and more effectively...I believe that a classical dance background is a must for the jazz dancer."

Dagmar Kossman
Teacher, Choreographer, Director
Velbert, West Germany

Thoughts on Jazz / 23

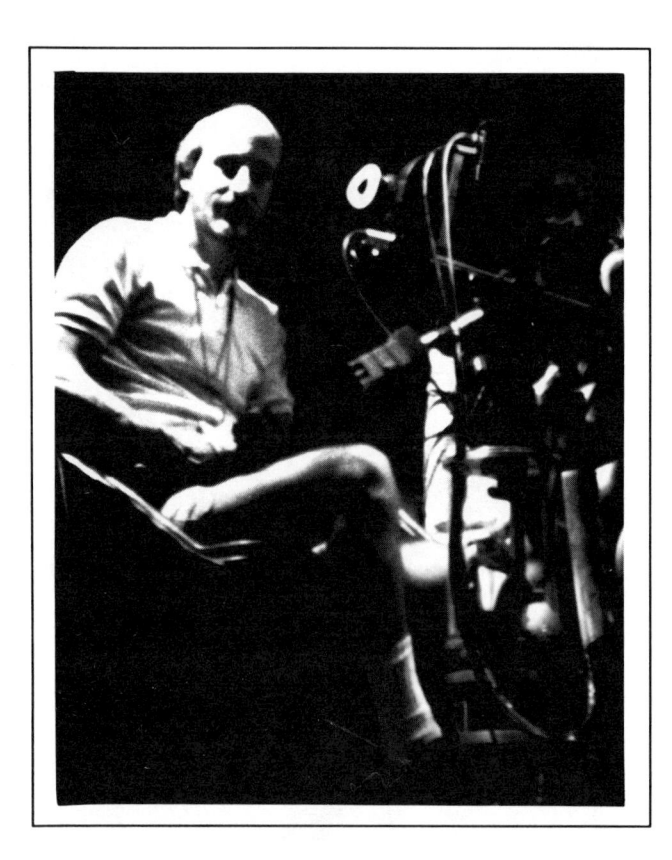

"With any kind of choreography, you must try to imitate life with a style and grace to entertain the viewer....Jazz dance gives you a caricature of an image and that image is background for the artist performing the song.

"Unlike classical forms of movement, Jazz dance within the Corporate/Industrial video world helps sell the message with a wider range of feelings. Jazz dance has that energy required for relaxing the corporate work force."

Herb Kossover
Director of Music Videos
Panther Productions, Inc.
Atlanta, GA

Photo: Steve Mitchell

" We need a new language for jazz dance — it's a word nearly as overused and misused as 'love' For instance, I have a hard time seeing the jazz influenced choreography being performed by ballet companies as jazz. The dancer trained for a lifetime to reach for the sky with every cell is the very antithesis of the dancer who trains herself or himself to manifest the earth directed impulses of jazz. So, that is not to say ballet dancers cannot work on jazz technique, but that we need more language to describe the synthesized forms that arise from jazz's influence."

T. Meriah Kruse
Teacher, Choreographer, Artistic Director: Syncopated, Inc.
Lexington, KY

"Life today is fast...Live fast and sometimes die fast...Have fun today for tomorrow may never come. However you think and live your life, there is a necessity to have a discipline, of a sort, if you wish to survive.

"Jazz dance is an expression of this kind of life. There is a joy and a pleasure in jazz dance, even as there is in jazz music, that you will not find in any other form of dance. There is a freedom, a liberation, that cannot be found in another style. In this freedom and liberation is a form of creativity. This creativity is a personal expression of individuality. This individuality is without limitation. This discipline, liberation, and freedom with limitation is 'jazz dance'...a true art form."

Matt Mattox
Choreographer, Master Teacher
France

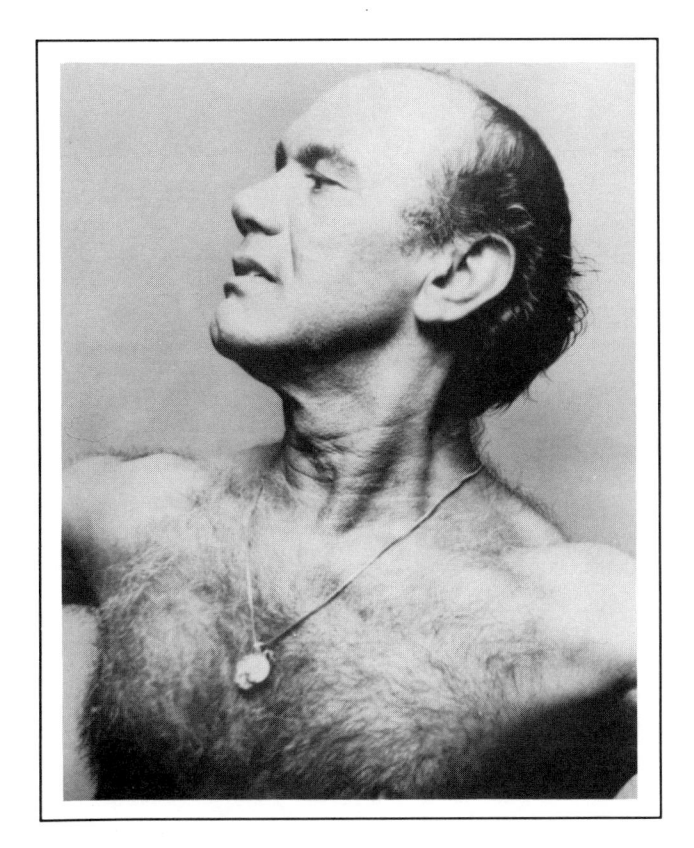

"Never Stop Moving!!!"

Luigi
Choreographer, Master Jazz Dance Teacher
New York

"Jazz dance is one of the great exports from the U.S.A. to the countries of the world. Its meld of African, Caribbean, and early Black dance is unique to this country. The first Jazz dance artists working the theatre used a minimum of dance vocabulary, movements that were exclusive to their individual physical abilities. Theatrical visionaries such as Katherine Dunham and Jack Cole added the technique of their classrooms to this wonderfully rhythmic and basically primitive dance. Theatre Jazz dance was born. Choreographers like Jerome Robbins carried it to high accomplishment. The great George Balanchine, in one of his teacher seminars, indicated that dance travels from the theatre to the classroom and only rarely the other way. So it has been with Jazz Dance. The time has come for codification."

Duncan Noble
Choreographer, Master Teacher
North Carolina

"Jazz dance teachers, dancers and choreographers would benefit greatly from exposing themselves to different teachers of this dance form. Basic techniques have been established, but the brilliance of this dance form is what can be developed from the technique."

Pattie Obey
Teacher, Choreographer
Amsterdam, Holland

" I believe that jazz dance training can be very important to all dancers...from your first class, jazz dance affords you the freedom to interpret and imprint your dancing with individual expression and your own personality."

Peter Powlus
Dancer, Teacher, Choreographer
Atlanta, GA

Photo: Heike Wippermann

"Afro Dance is an important training tool for a Jazz Dancer because it gives them a natural way of moving. Afro dance is rhythm of the heart, blood and soul."

Amparo Olmedo
Dancer, Teacher and Choreographer of Afro, Latin and Jazz
Cologne, West Germany and Biarritz, France

Photo: M. Hornschemeyer

"Jazz dance is a multi-cultural style that has great meaning for anyone involved in musicals, show dance or ballet schools. In Europe, it is its own art form though it is not as widely recognized as it is in its origin, America. There, more young dancers are in modern, jazz and ballet and the chance is also given for them to develop new forms for the theater. Instead of the traditional musicals, new multi-media shows are popping up which will bring new connections between dancing, singing and acting."

Gunther Rebel
Teacher, Choreographer, Director: Rebel Tanz
Munster, West Germany

Photo: Heike Wippermann

"It's interesting to see jazz dance in Europe grow in technique and thought. What a WONDERFUL art form!"

Petra Schulte-Kölpin
Teacher, Director: First Floor Tanz Studio
Hagen, West Germany

"I have seen jazz dance expand from the great Jack Cole to today's expressions of the art form. Today's students have a legacy of wealth to draw upon from our Jazz Dance Masters. Dance Educators of America Inc. has been fortunate to share with our membership these masters and to help promote disciples to carry on the art and progressions of jazz dance."

Vickie Sheer
Executive Director: Dance Educators of America

"True Jazz Dance is really about translating the rhythms found in classic jazz music into motion that sings through the body. Dancing is not primarily jazz because it looks like jazz, it's jazz because it sounds like the syncopations swinging musicians have been blowing off the bandstands for over half a century. It's the dance's articulation of offbeat accents in a swinging rhythm that endows it with a jazz feeling...."

Billy Siegenfield
*Teacher, Dancer, Choreographer,
Artistic Director: The Jump Rhythm Jazz Project
New York*

"As a teacher of Modern Dance around the world, I have been exposed to many different students of ranging dance disciplines. I found that, in the past, the jazz students lacked dramatic depth, but today, because, I feel, the jazz teacher has a wider range of dance disciplines, the jazz student is currently a dancer of great rank among those students that truly express themselves in movement. The growing use of the upper body in a fluid lyrical sense has given jazz choreography this wonderful feeling of true emotion that modern dance has always enjoyed.

"Jazz dance has definitely come around and into its own as a valid theatrical art form. Long gone are the days that the jazz dancer's only function was to 'sexually enhance' the appearance of a singer on a TV show. In the depths of the jazz dancer's soul, the scope of dramatic emotions have grown."

Bill Spencer
Teacher, Choreographer
Oregon and West Germany

"I look for dancers with Heart, Soul and Energy."

Delia Stewart
Teacher, Choreographer
Director: Delia Stewart Dance Company
Houston, Texas

Thoughts on Jazz / 30

"As director of Dance Olympus and as a convention teacher, I have watched the growth of Dance in America through the eyes of an administrator and an instructor. I have witnessed the American dancer embrace the classical training of ballet whose foundation began before the birth of our country; the multi-national amalgamation known as tap dance and the truly American dance form we call jazz.

"It is my feeling that knowledge of all of these forms begins and is fine tuned in the classroom of the dancing school.

"The convention class exposes the student to new teachers and new styles. It fosters quick learning and retention of material as well as healthy competition. The convention, coupled with good classroom training helps to expand and complete the development of the dance student."

Art Stone
Art Stone, Inc.
New York

"Jazz is a conglomerate of many things..primitive...Afro-Cuban...The Black Bottom...the Charleston...Swing Dance...Street Dance..Today...Ballet and Modern and so on...it is really the American Vernacular dance as expressed by the Stearns.

"Charlie Morrison, in the early fifties, discovered the name "modern Jazz" in the studio of Ernest Carlos at 52nd and Broadway. Charlie Morrison was teaching a style that evening that was always called 'Swing Dance,' style which characterized most black musicals and night club shows. It seems that all the dancers in Charlie's class were thrilled with this new and exciting dance style. 'What was it?' they asked in one voice. 'What is this thing we are feeling?'

"Always smart and sharp, Ernest had to have an answer to protect this new popular class. Looking down at the record player, he saw an album cover with the title 'The Modern Jazz Quartet'. Turning to the class Ernest yelled, 'Hey, man, this is modern jazz! Ain't it hot?'

"So help me, this is the true story as told to me by one of the dancers in the class.

"It is said that Jerome Robbins, one of the students in that class, took the spirit and feeling and produced the exciting choreography of 'West Side Story,' the first Broadway musical with the distinct label 'that is jazz.'

"I have seen it with my own eyes and experienced the birth and growth of Jazz. It is an old but new dance form born from the beat of the primitive drums emerging through the many facets of Black survival as a positive dance influence throughout the entire world."

Tommy Sutton
Tap Dancer, Teacher, Choreographer
Decatur, GA

"Dance is a universal language accessible to almost anybody...people find it easier to tune into Afro dance, jazz dance or even tap dance as these are based on rhythm and beat and natural motions accompanied by music that's just good fun."

Fred Traguth
*Teacher, Choreographer
Director: International Tanz Werkstatt
Bonn, West Germany*

"The great and ever growing appeal of jazz dance dictates a need for terminology! With the advent of music videos, a much larger portion of heretofore lay people are becoming introduced to various styles of jazz dance...creating a worldwide larger based interest group! The interest in jazz dance will continue to explode!"

Joe Tremaine
*Teacher, Choreographer
Van Nuys, CA*

Thoughts on Jazz / 32

" In the Jazz Dance form of this decade we have seen a very heavy physical, or aerobic influence, due to society's emphasis on physical fitness especially with our younger dancers. Now that this 'look' seems to be tiring somewhat, accomplished Jazz Dancers are returning to the 'tried and true' jazz dance forms utilizing music of even the 30's and 40's involving a greater showcase for their technique...

"As the pendulum swings back, our dancers can now better understand why this emphasis on technique has been necessary."

Dan Youmans
Dancer, Teacher, Choreographer
Artistic Director: Atlanta Jazz Theatre
Atlanta, GA

NOTES

Photo: Marden Photographers

CHAPTER 2

WHAT IS JAZZ DANCE?

Jazz Dance...what do we know about it? It has been said that if it isn't tap, ballet, or modern, then it must be jazz.

A search through local libraries turns up virtually nothing other than references to reviews of performances and performers. There is very little written about jazz dancing as an art form and what there is only covers the last half of the twentieth century.

Where did jazz dancing originate? While many of the movements have come from Ragtime and other popular dances, its roots are deep within the Negro culture, especially that of the African slaves. This is evident in the similarity of both the movements and accents.

While jazz dancing has become international in its growth and appeal, it is still typically American. Jazz is the mood of urban America: the stress, the humor, the romance, the excitement of the city.

Jazz is unpretentious and direct. Dance in general, is personal and is an effective means of communicating feelings. Jazz dancing takes self expression even further by allowing for greater creativity. There are fewer boundaries to limit the dancer which means that a work can utilize several different rhythms. The parameters are almost limitless and jazz dancing, by virtue of its nature, is exciting, electric, meaningful and fun. It is bright and creative. It is ever changing. Jazz is now.

Though it seems less structured than ballet, modern, and other forms of dance, there are still rules. It should not be assumed that jazz dance can be learned without formal, structured classes and education in its history. Just as speech has rules of grammar to ensure intelligent communication, before you can "say it in dance," you must first understand the meaning and proper execution of the movements.

Jazz is an art form that encompasses many schools of thought. In Jazz Danceology, we will explore these schools of thought and examine the various techniques and styles of jazz.

STYLES OF JAZZ DANCE

Jazz can be classified by style. I have identified what I consider to be the major styles. This is not to say that these are the only styles, but that they are the primary ones. They are the most distinctive and from which spring the variations yet, these styles are not unrelated. Often there are similarities between them and there is a great deal of overlapping.

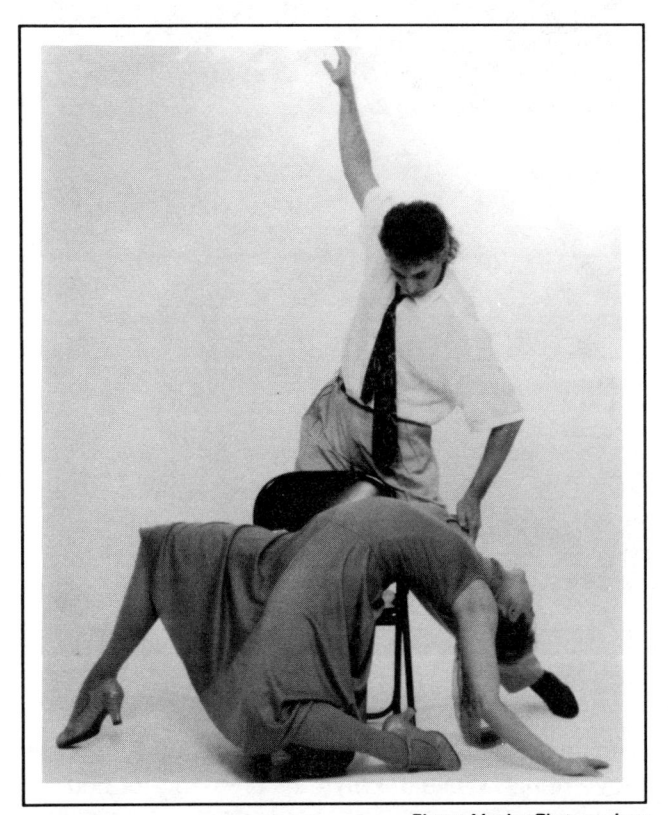

Photo: Marden Photographers

THE BLUES

Blues is in the blood stream of the jazz dancer..the feeling deep down. It is the slow drag, the lethargic, languid movements. It is snake hips, oozing - descending from the mournful, oppressive mood of the Negro spiritual. Examples of Blues are found in *Porgy and Bess* and *Black and Blue*.

Photo: Mike Canale

LYRICAL

Lyrical is usually very "body line" oriented. Lyrical is very similar to ballet in that it is flowing and graceful. The movements may be performed in an adagio (slow) manner. *Cats* has many examples of Lyrical Jazz.

Photo: Marden Photographers

BROADWAY/THEATRICAL

This is also called Musical Theatre dance. In this form, jazz dance can tell a story. At times Theatrical dancing will use highly stylized movements and comedy to support its form. When we refer to dance as being stylized, we are talking about the choreographer's style. (Fosse, Bennet, Robbins, Tune, etc.) We can look at a dance and know immediately who choreographed it. Examples of Broadway/Theatrical are found in " Slaughter on Tenth Avenue" from *On Your Toes* choreographed by Balanchine.

Photo: Marden Photographers

"HOT"

"Hot Jazz" is full of high stepping, excited movements. While the rhythms are exaggerated, the posture may include a slouched back, swinging hips and shrugging shoulders. This is normally the form of jazz we associate with television or videos, commercial in its intent. "Hot Jazz" is also a great form of entertainment. Examples of "Hot Jazz" can be found in *Dancin* by Fosse.

What is Jazz Dance? / 38

Photo: Marden Photographers

MODERN JAZZ

This popular art form is effortless and improvisational. It is closer to modern dance than to ballet though it is a blend of both forms in both intent and movement. The movements seem to originate in the pelvic area and often appear sensual and sometimes even sexual. This form of jazz has the quality of driving insistence while at the same time, relaxed informality. We can see examples of Modern Jazz in the performances of the Alvin Ailey Dance Company.

"COOL"

This form of jazz is smooth and also highly stylized taking on the distinct characteristics of the choreographer. What makes it "cool", however, is the music. An excellent example of this style is the "Cool" dance from *West Side Story*. A second example is the *N.Y. Export Opus Jazz* by Jerome Robbins.

Joel Hall Photo: Ken Duncan

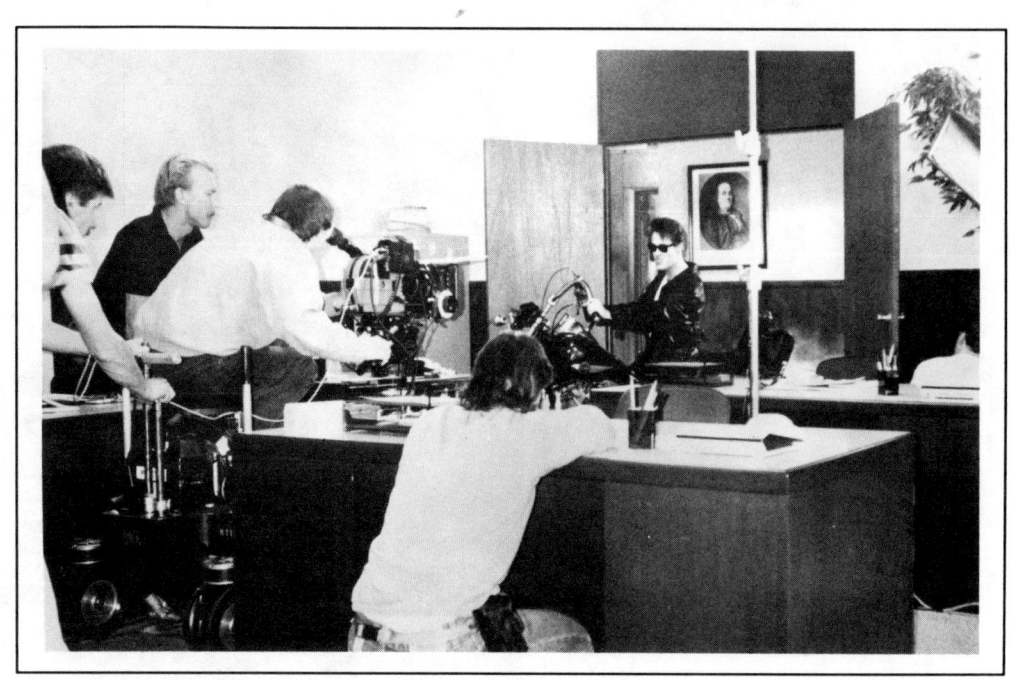

Photo: Creative Edge, Atlanta, GA

WEST COAST

This is one of the latest forms to emerge on the jazz dance scene. West coast is composed of elements of the other styles but is usually more up beat and a bit "hotter". West Coast is found in rap videos and includes elements of street dancing and break dancing.

ROCK

Rock is a loose, more percussive style of jazz. It is based on creativity and a feeling for both the music and the movement. Rock emerged in the '60's and has the look of that era. *Grease* has examples of Rock.

Photo: Mike Canale

What is Jazz Dance? / 40

Photo: Helke Wippermann

AFRO-JAZZ

Afro-Jazz uses fewer terms in its study than most other jazz forms. Its roots are clearly found in the study of African Dance. Afro-Jazz is distinguishable by its emphasis on rhythms and feelings. It seems to return to the native style and is not as commercialized as other forms of jazz. Afro-Jazz can be incorporated into other styles of jazz dancing. Examples of Afro-Jazz can be found in certain selections of Dance Theater of Harlem and some of Alvin Ailey's performances.

Photo: Marden Photographers

LATIN

Latin is a dance style from Latin America and includes the Cha Cha, Mambo, Samba, Tango, etc. As in Afro-Jazz, the rhythms are distinctive. The accompanying music is of the same format.

Latin style can be seen in *Dirty Dancing*, the dance, "America" from the movie *West Side Story*, as well as many of Fred Astaire's movies.

CALYPSO (Carribean)

Though Calypso is similar to and often categorized as Latin, there are some very real differences. The rhythms are very much alike yet, where Latin utilizes accents and percussive movements, Calypso is smooth and flowing. Calypso was popularized in the 60's and 70's by singer, Harry Belafonte. In Calypso, if the right hip accents, the right shoulder accents, etc. using the same isolations as walks. Examples of Calypso can be seen in Garth Fagan's *From Before*.

Photo: Frank Gimpaya

OTHER

Other jazz styles exist in combined forms. For example, Tap/Jazz, Jazz/Ballet (classical), Cabaret which is similar to Musical Theater/Comedy Dance, and Social Dance, the dancing we do with partners at social gatherings. We might also mention here some of the temporary styles such as disco, break dancing, and the Lindy. Though they are fads which come and go, often rather swiftly, they contain elements of and contribute elements to the more established styles.

These other forms play an important role in jazz dance. They are often the foundation for dance in Broadway shows, television, concert dance and movies.

Even though we have presented and labeled the styles as different, they are similar in many ways and share the common characteristics of distinguishable rhythms and movements that communicate feelings.

CHAPTER 3
TERMINOLOGY and TECHNIQUE

With proper technique, one can move freely and more confidently. As we say in dance, "Technique is Freedom."

Because we have so much terminology in dance it has been said that we have our own language. Perhaps this is true. The terminology is universal and the abbreviations are consistent from locale to locale. It is important to recognize them and learn the most frequently used terms and abbreviations. The more familiar you are with the dancers' language, the easier it will be for you to read and understand notes, choreography, and text on dance.

It is also important that you teach both the terminology and their meanings to your students. For example, développé means "to develop." Familiarization with the meanings makes the execution easier.

A SPECIAL NOTE ON TEACHING PLACEMENT...

Research has shown that the two main causes of dance (and athletic) injuries are improper placement and improper warm up.

Placement is very important when teaching all forms of dance yet, in jazz dance, placement is sometimes overlooked. The focus seems to be more on style and feeling rather than on correct alignment. Perhaps this is because jazz seems so "urgent" and "today" and less traditional than its predecessors. Yet, proper alignment is crucial. It allows the body to execute an exercise or movement with greater ease while avoiding the possibility of injury. Because in jazz dance our movements and positions can be complicated, we, as teachers, must be educated and be able to teach our students about proper placement.

Proper placement is easily achieved through what I refer to as the "**Plumb Line**" method. This is simply lining the body on a straight line. A Plumb Line is used in other professions to achieve a straight line and I have used it in dance to align the dancer's body. It is a visual concept that the students can easily understand. The body is centered (lying down, standing, or moving) with the ear over the shoulder, the shoulder over the rib cage, the rib cage over the pelvis, the pelvis over the knees, and the knees over the feet.

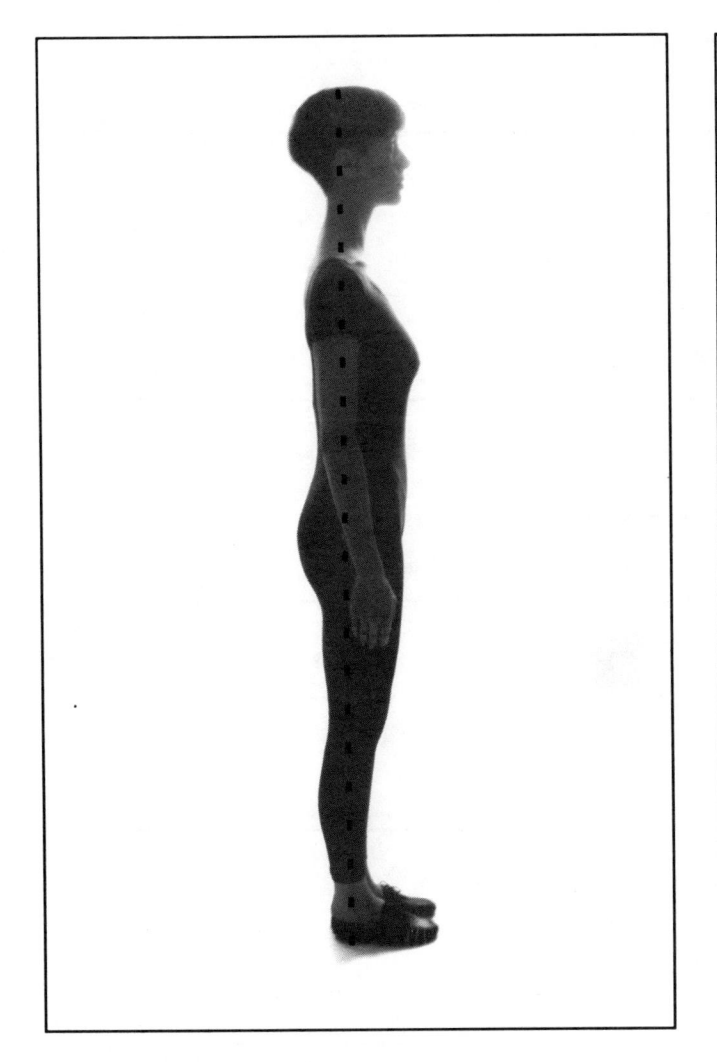

"Plumb Line" method - This illustrates a plumb line from ear to ankle. Note that the dancer is slightly forward, ready for movement forward, to the side, back, up, or down.

It is as though a line were dropped from the ear down the body to the foot. If the body is in alignment, it will line up on the imaginary plumb line in both parallel and turned out positions. The two most "out of order" areas of the body in jazz are the lower back (pelvic area) and the extended rib cage. It is important to pay close attention to these two areas when working on technique.

Teaching proper placement of the lower back and extended rib cage is essential. Correct placement is crucial from the opening exercise or movement of the class to the very last step.

This illustrates the **"Plumb Line"** method being pushed or tested. Note that the dancer has three of the five key spots in line: the shoulder, hip, and ankle. The ear, rib cage, and knees are out of line.

GENERAL TERMINOLOGY

The following terms refer to locations for exercises:

Barre - A horizontal bar where exercises are done. The barre is normally attached to the wall but can be free standing.

Center Barre - In the center of the floor. Center Barre refers to exercises traditionally done at a barre (such as tendu) but because they are done in the center or the floor, they are done without the barre.

Floor Work - On the floor.

Across the Floor - Where locomotive movements are done. These include leaps, runs, walks, turns and large combinations.

Note: In the following sections, I frequently refer to ballet terms therefore, for your convenience, I have included a dictionary of those ballet terms most often used in Jazz dance terminology – See Appendix.

GENERAL TERMS USED IN JAZZ DANCE

Barrel Turn (as in tap dance) - Head stays forward as the body rotates around it. This can be done in the air. For example, parallel pas de chat.

Terminology and Technique / 47

General Terms - Continued

Body Roll - Begin with the knees bent and roll up to head. A body roll can go all or part way up to the head.

1

2

3

4

Terminology and Technique / 48

General Terms - Continued

Bridge (also called a back bend) - This is an exercise that is gymnastic in nature and is great for the back. There are 3 degrees of bridges:

1

2

Bridge — 1st degree - Lie on back, feet in 2nd position parallel. Arch the back and support body on shoulders. A variation is to grasp the ankles as the back arches.

1

2

Bridge — 2nd degree - Lie on back, feet are in 2nd position parallel. Hands are next to the ears on either side of the head. Using hands and feet, push up to straight arms.

General Terms - Continued

Bridge — 3rd Degree - This is very advanced. Lie on back, feet are in 2nd position parallel, back is arched toward ceiling, arms are straight and the weight is supported on the hands and feet. Leg is lifted into passé neutral and développés to the ceiling.

1

2

General Terms - Continued

Bridge — 3rd Degree – Variation: When développé to ceiling, bring leg down to knee on floor with foot toward back of head. Return to passé and bring foot back to floor. Can be done either right or left. While knee is down, push against floor, rise up to both knees, and arch to knees. Hands leave floor and reach forward.

Terminology and Technique / 51

General Terms - Continued

Chest Lift - Floor exercise with back on the floor. The chest releases and lifts off the floor toward the ceiling (or to full sitting position.)

Chug - A short sliding hop or jump into the floor with heels following the balls of the feet and accenting on the heel. Accent can be heavy or light. The chug is most often found in tap dancing.

Compass Turn - Like an arabesque turn but the toe of the working leg remains on the floor (like a compass that a student uses in mathematics class.) This turn is often preceded or followed by a paddle turn.

General Terms - Continued

Contract(ion) - To pull in, as in contraction of the stomach or other body part. To hollow out, to bring together.

1

2

Crab Walk - Walk to front, side or back with body in Table Top (see Table Top) position on hands and feet, body facing ceiling.

Double Attitude Jump or Leap - Jumping or leaping in an open swastika (open 4th).

Double Time - Twice as fast as the tempo of the music.

Terminology and Technique / 53

General Terms - Continued

Fan Kick - This is done with a straight leg. Cross leg over body and lift it straight toward the head. Leg makes a swooping circular pattern across the body and completes the circle on the other side of the body. The path of the leg resembles a fan.

Terminology and Technique / 54

General Terms - Continued

1 *2* *3*

Flat Back (also called Table Top) - A position in which the back is flat, like a table. There are various degrees of flat back. Parallel to the floor and 45 degrees up or down are the most common. Flat back is most frequently performed standing or on hands and knees (torso facing floor). It is also done with hands and feet on floor and body raised facing the ceiling.

4 *5*

Terminology and Technique / 55

General Terms - Continued

Flea Hop or Flea Slide - Sliding or hopping on a diagnal in passé position (turned out, turned in, or neutral.)

Flick - Accent quickly as with hands or feet.

Frog (also called Butterfly) - Sitting or lying down, knees are bent with the soles of the feet together or toes pointed and big toes touching. This is good to develop flexibility in the hips.

Half Time - Half as fast as the tempo of the music.

General Terms - Continued

Horseshoe - An open ballet (classical) attitude shaped like a horseshoe from the top. Lean away from the attitude and toward the supporting leg.

ISOLATIONS

Moving one body part such as the head, shoulder, rib cage or hip independently from the rest of the body.

ISOLATION — Hands and Arms (port de bras)

Airplane - Both hands are extended in 2nd position so that when the body turns, it resembles an airplane.

Baseball Bat - Hands are clasped together as if holding a baseball bat. The "bat" can be either swinging or at the shoulder ready to hit.

Bow and Arrow - A position of the arms resembling shooting a bow and arrow. One arm is bent at the elbow, the other is extended. Hands can be jazz hands, fists, etc.

Isolation / Hands and Arms - Continued

Comb - Spread the fingers and comb the hair close to the sides of the head.

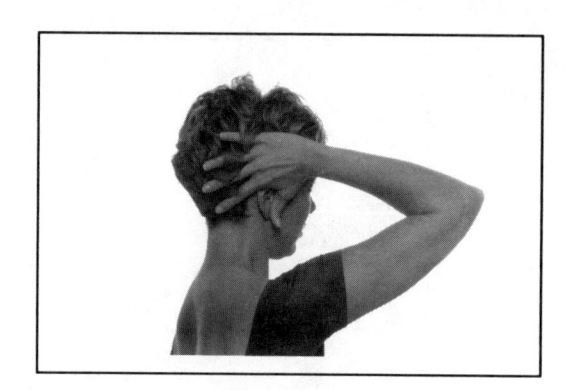

Drape - Arm is relaxed and hanging across the head.

Terminology and Technique / 58

Isolation / Hands and Arms - Continued

1 *2* *3*

Finger Fan - Beginning with the little finger, rolling the fingers in toward the body then back out.

Fist - Hand is clenched into a tight ball.

Jazz Frame - Arms are crossed over the head making an "X". Fingers are spread into jazz hands.

Terminology and Technique / 59

Isolation / Hands and Arms – Continued

Jazz Hands (Giordano technique) - The fingers are spread. Do not fan them back.

Jazz Wrist Press - Flexing the hand at the wrist, push the palm and wrist away from the shoulder in any direction. This can be done with a jazz hand or relaxed fingers.

"L" - One arm is extended up to ceiling, the other arm is extended to the side forming an "L." Hands can be in various positions.

Isolation / Hands and Arms - Continued

Long Jazz Arm (Giordano technique) - Like ballet 2nd position but arm is straighter. When seated upright or standing, palms are facing the floor.

"S" Curve - A position in which the arms are to the sides and lifted away from the body with one arm rounded up and the other rounded down to form an "S."

Scoop - A scooping motion with the arm rounded and hand cupped.

Second Position (as in ballet) - The arms reach to the sides from the shoulders and are slightly forward. Palms are forward.

Isolation / Hands and Arms – Continued

Shampoo (from West Coast Style) - Bring the rounded arm around the top of the head in a circular motion touching the finger across the head to the opposite ear.

1

2

3

4

Slice - Arm makes a cutting motion through the air. Hand is usually flat like a knife.

Isolation / Hands and Arms – Continued

"V" Position - Arms are extended up in a "V" with palms facing either in or out. This is a very strong line.

Windmill - A motion resembling a windmill. Right arm is extended up, left arm is down to the floor. Left arm makes a circle up while right arm makes a circle down continuing through to the beginning position. (Can be reversed.) This is combined with a body turn, often a barrel or two step turn.

Wrist Roll - Hand rotates freely in or out. This can be done with open hand or closed fist.

Terminology and Technique / 63

General Terms - Continued

ISOLATION - Head

Contract - Bring the chin toward the chest. Continue to focus forward.

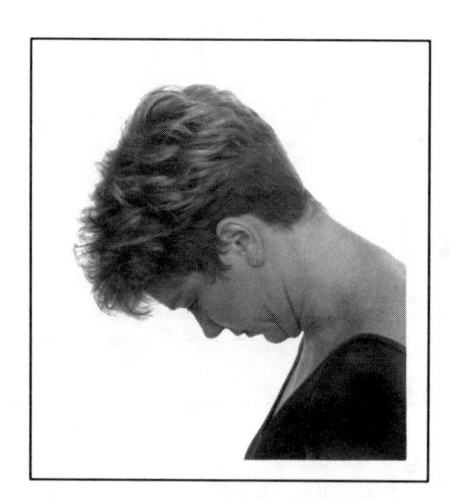

Goose Neck (chicken neck) - Head pushes (pulses) forward and contracts back.

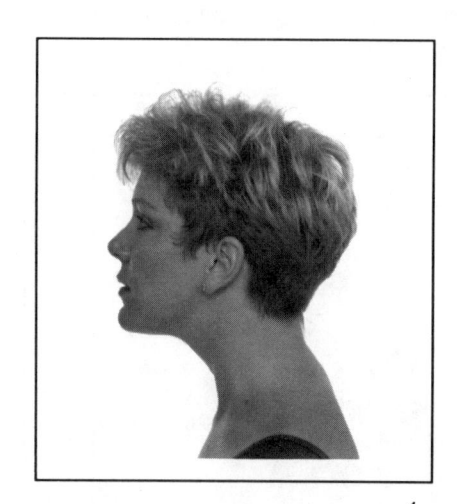

1

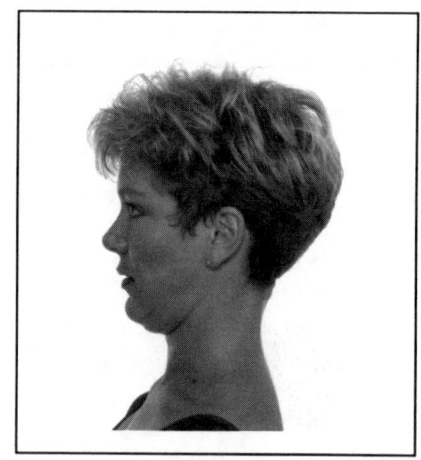

2

Profile - With body forward, face extreme right or extreme left.

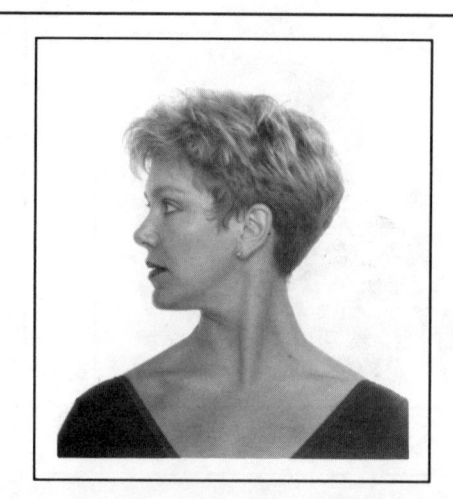

Terminology and Technique / 64

Isolation / Head – Continued

Release - Push the head back toward the ceiling. Continue to focus forward.

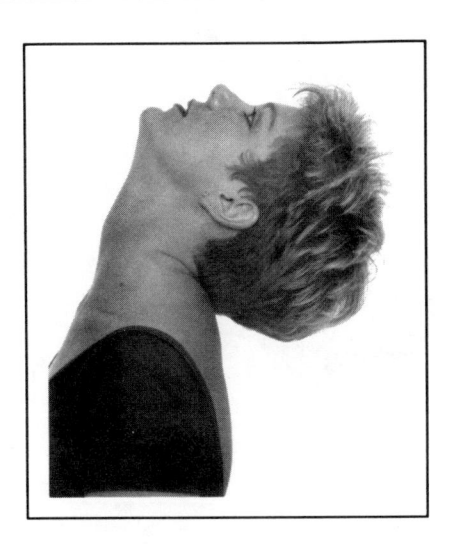

Roll - Drop head down to right, roll to left continuing in a circle or drop down to left, roll to right continuing in a circle. Face forward. It is not necessary to go backward or return to starting point.

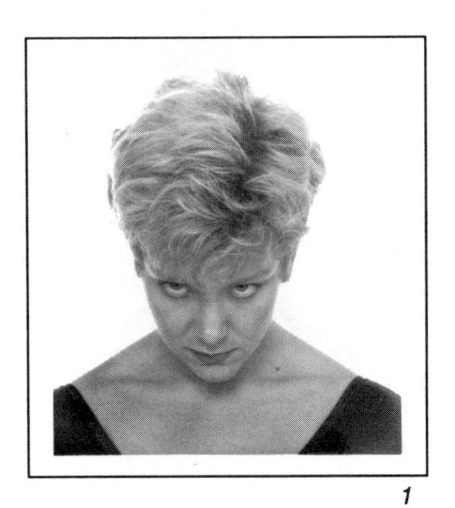

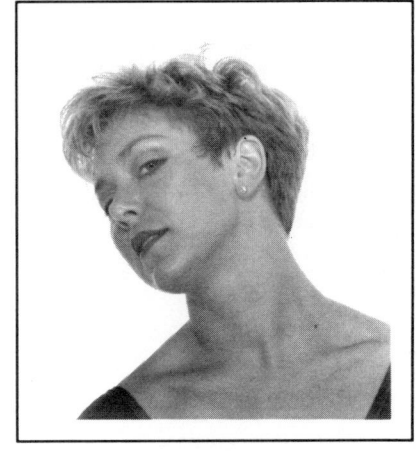

Terminology and Technique / 65

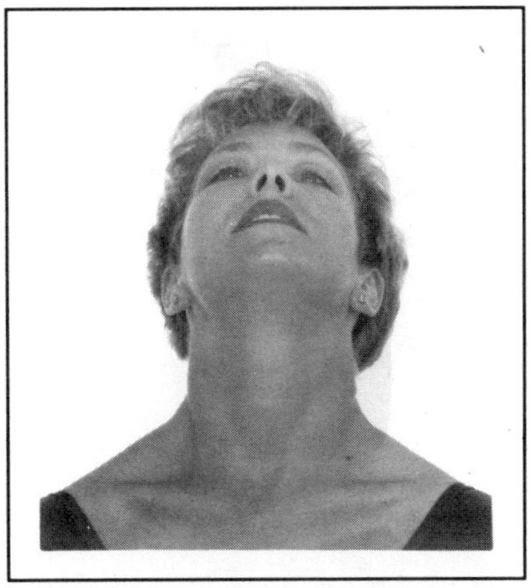

Isolation / Head – Continued

Side to Side - Very East Indian in style and movement. Isolate the head laterally while facing forward.

1

2

Swing - Drop head right, swing down to left and hold or drop left down to right and hold. Face forward. (Similar to a roll but head doesn't make a complete circle.)

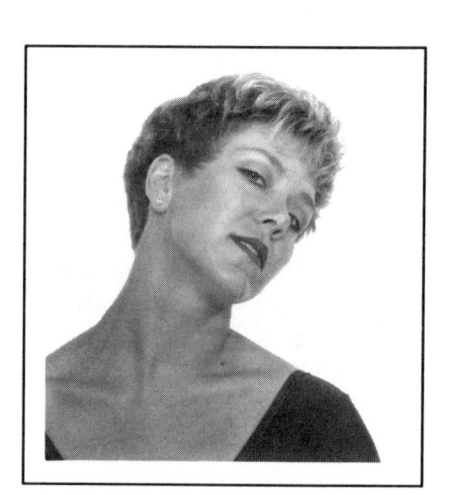

1

2

Tilt - Tilt head to the side while facing (focusing) forward.

General Terms - Continued

ISOLATION - Hips

Contract - Tuck pelvis under and lengthen back.

Hip Lift - Lift hip up or to the side. Can be done in various positions however, the most common is passé neutral.

Isolation / Hips – Continued

Release - Push buttocks back and arch lower back. Can be performed in various degrees.

Roll - Can be either right or left. For example: left hip starts and moves in circular pattern to front, right, back and returns to starting point. When reading notes, remember to start opposite side. That is, to roll right, begin left.

Side to Side - Accenting hip pulses to side in either single or double time.

Swivel - Rotate the direction you step. Step right, rotate right; step left, rotate left.

General Terms - Continued

ISOLATION - Rib Cage

Contract - Open shoulder blades while closing front of the rib cage. Do not use shoulders.

Diagonal Pulse - With body facing corner, push the rib cage toward the corner of the room. Pulse may be in different rhythms.

Release - Push ribs (chest) forward. Keep hips and shoulders stationary.

Isolation / Rib Cage - Continued

Rib Cage Roll - Roll right or left in a full circle.

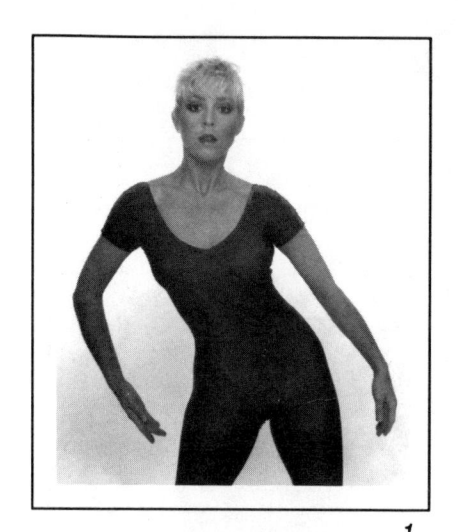

1

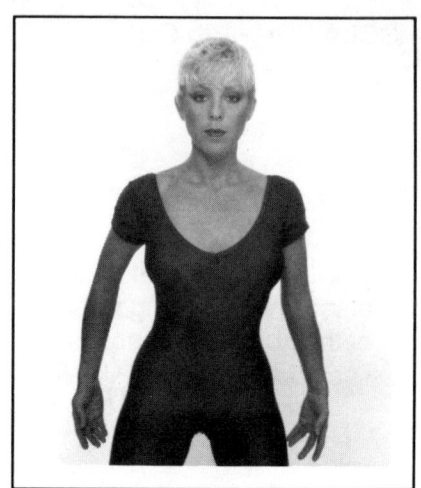

2

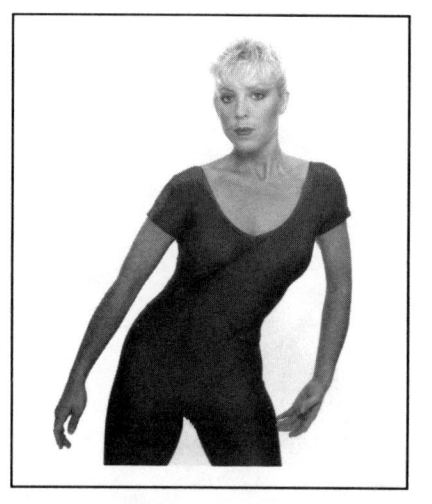

3

4

Rib Cage Side - Shift rib cage to right or left.

Rib Cage Square - Move rib cage in a square. It can be front, side, back, side, or side, back, side, front.

General Terms - Continued

ISOLATION - Shoulders

Back - A thrusting motion back.

Front - A thrusting motion forward.

Roll - Either front or back in a circular motion.

Terminology and Technique / 71

Isolation / Shoulders - Continued

Shimmy - Shake shoulders quickly alternating forward and back. That is, right shoulder back while left is forward etc..

1

2

Up/Down - Pull shoulder(s) up toward ear and push them back down without moving the head.

1

2

General Terms - Continued

Jack Knife - A position of the arms. From second position bend arms at the elbows bringing hands across the front of the chest. Hands can be in fists, wrist press, palms down, etc.

Variation: From second position, the elbows come together in front of the chest with arms at a 45 degree angle to each other. Hands can be fists, jazz hands etc.

General Terms - Continued

Jazz Pas de Bourrée - May be done under (back) or over (forward). This is usually taught as step cross, step open, step open. This is used for movements across the floor or preparations for turns, jumps and leaps. Begin standing with one leg free to execute the move.

1

2

3

4

General Terms - Continued

Jazz Split - Front leg is straight while the back leg is bent and behind the hip. Back leg should be in line with the hip. This may be used in floor exercises and in leaps.

Split

General Terms - Continued

Jazz Square - Can be open or crossed. Step right cross over, left back, right side, left forward making a square or reverse by starting with left cross over. You can also begin stepping side first.

1

2

3

4

5

Terminology and Technique / 76

General Terms - Continued

JAZZ WALKS AND JAZZ RUNS

(Note that some will use more style than technique and vice versa.) - Jazz walks and runs can be done with almost any hand position that works for your choreography: shampoo with Cuban (as in Cha-Cha-Cha), jazz hands with low walks, etc.

Camel Walk - An older style walk often seen in social dancing during the height of the swing era. It is a walk with the opposite hip lifted. For example, step right, left hip up, step left, right hip up.

Variations: In place, moving front, or moving sideways

Terminology and Technique / 77

Jazz Walks and Jazz Runs - Continued

Cha-Cha-Cha - Like a Latin walk but counted: 1 and 2 or 3 and 4, etc. Cha-Cha-Cha is step, step, step with alternating feet and can move to the side, forward, or back. As in the social dance, it is the Cha-Cha-Cha step of the Cha Cha. An example of this step is found in the dance, "America" from *West Side Story* Mambo, Samba and other Latin rhythms are similar. The Mambo, for example, is counted: step 1, hold 2, step 3,4. It may be done front, side or back. The Samba is counted: step front 1 and 2 and, back 3 and 4. This may also be done to the side.

Chassé - This means "chase" and may be done in any direction depending on your choreography. In the chassé, the legs come together. They do not cross. Chassé is counted 1 and 2. Step right, slide left leg to right, step right open, slide left leg to right. This is also a preparation move.

1

2

3

Terminology and Technique / 78

Jazz Walks and Jazz Runs - Continued

Cuban or Latin - Push opposite hip to the side as you step. Step right, push hip left, step left, push hip right. Cuban is also an example of style more than technique.

1

2

3

4

Terminology and Technique / 79

Jazz Walks and Jazz Runs - Continued

Grapevine - Used to travel. Normally this is performed facing the audience. Step right side, cross left back, step right side, step left front. This can also begin with step cross in front. The origin of the grapevine is in folk dancing.

1

2

3

4

5

Jazz Walks and Jazz Runs - Continued

High and/or Vegas - Step right, cross left through passé in relevé with body lifted. This is an elegant walk in which the torso remains stationary. It is called Vegas because it resembles the walk of the show girls with big head dresses and heavy costumes. It is a walk with more style than technique.

1   2

Jazz Pas de Bourrée(s) - (p. 74)

Jazz Square - (p. 76)

Jazz Triplet - (p. 100)

Kimbo - This is a traditional jazz walk and though it is called a walk, it is actually fairly stationary. Step back right bending the knee. Keep left leg straight. Flex left foot keeping heel close to or on the floor. Repeat with left foot back and right foot flexed. Kimbo must go either to the side or back.

Terminology and Technique / 81

Jazz Walks and Jazz Runs - Continued

Low Jazz Run or Low Jazz Walk - These are the most basic of all the runs or walks in jazz dance. They are also called drag walks or drag runs. It is important to remain in plié as you walk or run. Step through 1st into 4th. Turn out should be comfortable unless the choreography dictates full turn out or even no turn out. Examples of low jazz walks are found in much of the choreography of *West Side Story*.

1

2

Spider - Plié relevé on one leg. Turn the back leg to attitude with opposite arm forward. This is repeated across the floor within combinations. The Spider is an example of technique more than style.

1

2

Jazz Walks and Jazz Runs - Continued

Spiral - The torso rotates around the pelvis (hips) while doing a high or low jazz walk. Spiral is an example of technique.

1

2

Step Ball Change - Used for preparation, to change feet, or to change weight to the other side.

1

2

3

Terminology and Technique / 83

Jazz Walks and Jazz Runs - Continued

Strut - A "hot" or "cool" walk. It is very stylized and may be performed in various ways. The basic strut (with body facing forward or to the corner) is step right open, step left cross, step right open, step left cross accenting up on the odd number counts. A strut can also be combined with an isolation.

Swivel - Here the action is in the hip. The hip rotates as you turn toward the supporting leg. This is not a pivot but a two step action. Step on right leg, left hip swivels toward left leg. (This is opposite of the Cuban walk which is step left, swivel left hip, etc.) The swivel resembles a belly dance or hula motion. It is also very WEST COAST in style.

General Terms - Continued

Knee Hinge - Standing, knees are bent and at a 45 degree angle (or lower) to the floor, hinging from the knee to the head. The body is in line (straight line) from the head, shoulders, rib cage, and pelvis to the knees. Do not arch. This can also be done on the knees. It is important to keep the back straight.

LAYOUTS

Layout-Back - The lower part of the back arches. The leg is in front and arms are usually in an open "V" back.

Layout - Continued

Layout - Front - There are two ways to do a front layout. The arms are not key here and can be in any of a number of aesthetically or physically comfortable positions.

(1) In 2nd position, leg is turned in, the body flat forward. For example, standing on right foot, left leg is lifted directly to side and turned in. The lifted foot is in line with the head

(2) The leg is back in arabesque with the body flat forward.

Layout - Side - Like a développé or battement in 2nd but the hip is lifted and the body is leaning away from the lifted leg. Lifted leg should be turned out as much as possible. A slight turn in may be necessary to achieve this line. Arms can be in 2nd, high 5th, in a "V," or they can be asymmetrical.

General Terms - Continued

Lindy - A jitterbug like movement. Chassé to the side with a ball change back. (Chassé, chassé, ball change or tap step, tap step, ball change.)

Locomotive Movements - Walks, runs, jumps, gallops, hops, leaps, skips, and slides.

Neutral - Where legs, head, or the entire body is in place facing forward. Example: passé neutral with no turn out.

General Terms - Continued

Passé Neutral Hip Lift - While leg is in passé neutral, hip is lifted to the side.

Perch - The body is in the same position as in a stag leap but on the floor.

1

2

General Terms - Continued

Pivot - Step forward right and without moving the left (supporting) leg from its position, turn back with left foot to complete motion. Can also be done stepping left and pivoting right.

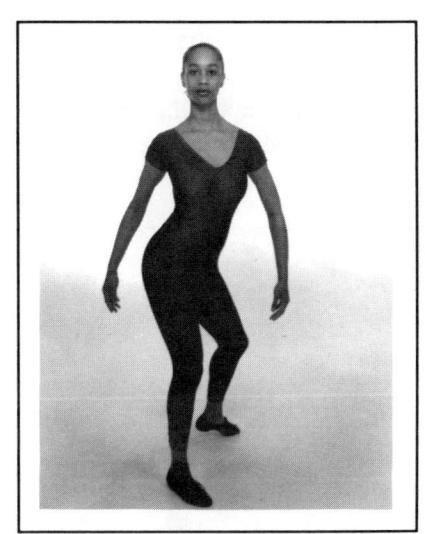

1

2

3

4

5

Terminology and Technique / 89

General Terms - Continued

Plié - 1st, 2nd, 3rd 4th and 5th positions. Plié can be done turned out or parallel (no turn out.) Sometimes the choreography may call for one foot turned in and one foot parallel. This imbalance can result in a jazzier look.

1st position turned out

1st position no turn out

1st position plié relevé turned out

2nd position turned out

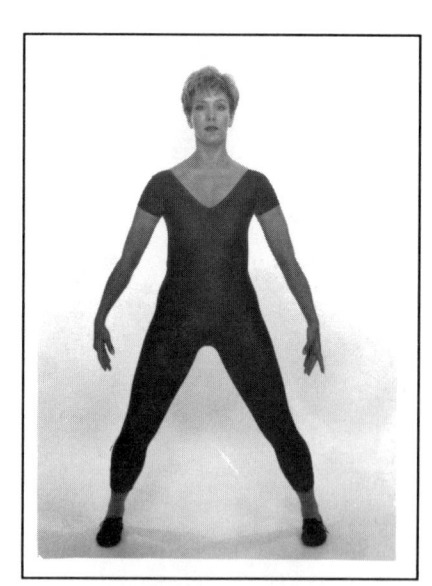

2nd position no turn out

2nd position plié relevé no turn out

Plié - Continued

3rd position turned out

4th position turned out

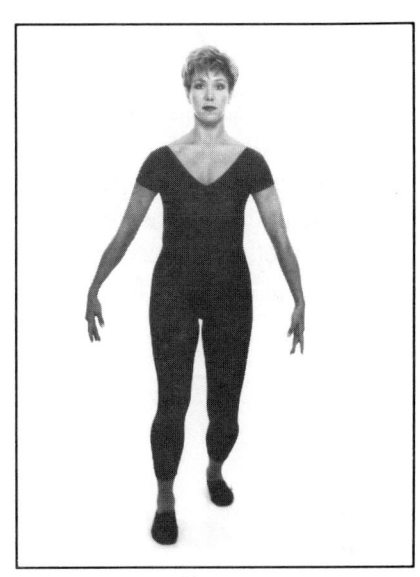

4th position no turn out

5th position turned out

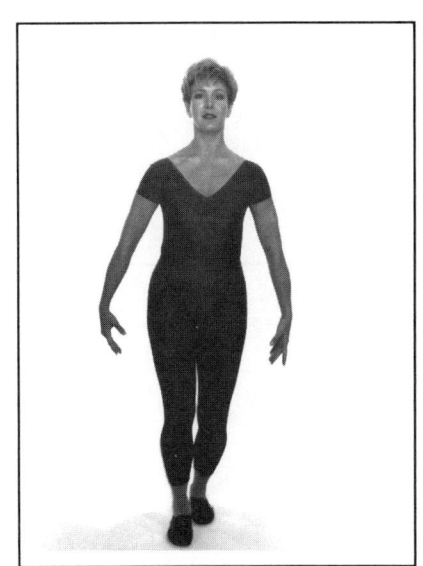

5th position no turn out

5th position plié relevé turned out

Terminology and Technique / 91

General Terms - Continued

Plié Relevé - This is a combination of a plié and a relevé. It is a plié on half toe which forces the arch of the foot. It is important to keep the heel over the toes.

Plow or Up and Over - Begin on the floor. Sit straight with legs straight in front. The back goes down to the floor and the legs (remaining straight, if possible,) go over and behind the head. This exercise is excellent for stretching out the lower back. Caution, however, on how the exercise is taught. Most believe that only advanced dancers should take the legs over straight.

Release - To relax, push up or forward. To arch.

1

2

General Terms - Continued

Roll Up - To uncurl, usually from a standing position. The body is either in a flat back parallel to the floor or relaxed over. Hands are on the floor if possible. Allow the lower stomach to begin this movement.

1

2

3

4

Russian Jump - Also called a toe touch jump or spread eagle. It is performed in 2nd position.

General Terms - Continued

Scoop and Press - Reaching the arm(s) forward or toward the feet or designated point, rise up to sitting or straight position. If standing, arms reach to 5th and push down to 2nd.

1

2

3

4

General Terms - Continued

Shoulder Stand - This is very advanced and requires stomach and back strength to execute. The body is supported on the shoulders on the floor. This is used in several jazz dance exercises as well as in modern.

Snap Kick - A quick développé kick, usually low (also called a flick kick.) Snap kicks are often used in '50's style choreography.

General Terms - Continued

Spiral - The torso rotates around the pelvis (hips).

Square (as in exercises) - Sitting with legs forward and body upright at 90 degree angle to the floor.

Stag (as in leap, jump or hop) - Forward leg is in passé with no turn out and the back leg is turned out in attitude.

Terminology and Technique / 96

General Terms - Continued

Sugar Foot - With feet in small second, swivel on the toes from side to side. This can also be done with one foot.

1

2

Swastika (as in Giordano Technique) - While sitting, the legs are in 4th position and both are bent. It is important that the hips are down and buttocks are on the floor. The heel of the front foot is in line with the center of the body. Some dancers have tight hips and must bring up the front knee to keep the back leg and buttocks on the floor.

General Terms - Continued

**Swastika - Continued
Variation:** Crossed Swastika (as in Giordano Technique) - Start in swastika. Bring back leg over front with foot on floor and knee up. Again, as in swastika, hips must be down and buttocks on the floor.

Switch Leap - In mid-air, at the highest point of the leap, the front leg switches to the back. There are several ways to do this:

a. straight leg passing from front to back
b. leg passing through passé from front to back
c. performing the movement in double attitude
d. passing leg from front to side

Table Top - A position in which the back or legs remain flat resembling a table. This can be done several ways and is used in a variety of movements including contractions, flat back standing and on the floor, and exercises for knee placement.

a. **Legs** - Sit on buttocks. With legs lifted, bend knees and keep shins straight and parallel to the floor.

Terminology and Technique / 98

General Terms - Continued

Table Top - Continued
  b. **Back** -
   (1.) Either standing or on hands and knees, the back is straight and parallel to the floor.

   (2.) This can also be done on hands and feet with the back to the floor and the body toward the ceiling. (This is not to be confused with a Bridge in which the back arches.)

General Terms - Continued

Triplet (Jazz Dance) - Triplet refers to movement of the feet counted 1 and 2. The major functions of triplets are traveling, changing weight from one foot to the other, and changing levels (such as up, up, down.) The feet (legs) should pass each other during the movement as in walk forward or back.

1

2

3

4

General Terms - Continued

Turned In Attitude - An attitude in which the leg is turned in from the hips.

"V" Position - Arms, legs, or entire body can be extended into a "V". Arms can be in "V" over the head or in front of the body with flat back. With back on the floor or from a seated position, legs can be raised in a "V" and can be either parallel or turned out. Body can be in a "V" with arms and legs straight and lifted to form a "V" with the buttocks on the floor. Here, too, the legs can be either parallel or turned out.

Variation:
Torso remains erect with arms in high second. Legs are in second position "V" off the floor.

General Terms - Continued

PREPARATIONS

A preparation is a technique or move that leads into or sets up the body for another move. For example, a plié in preparation for a jump. These suggested preparations will give height, momentum, and better placement to execute jumps, leaps, hops, or turns.

For directions/explanations of each technique refer to pages listed below.

Assemblé (p. 104)
Chassé (p. 78)
Compass Turn (p. 52, 113)
Crossed Swastika (p. 98)
Fan Kick (p. 54)
Flea Hop or Slide (p. 56)

Grapevine (p. 80)
Horseshoe (p. 57)
Jazz Pas de Bourrée (p. 74)
Jazz Split (p. 75)
Jazz Square (p. 76)
Pivot (p. 89)

Plié (p. 90, 91)
Plié Relevé (p. 92)
Step Ball Change (p. 83)
Swastika (p. 97)
Triplet (p. 100)

General Terms - Continued

JUMPS, LEAPS, AND HOPS

See notes on Terminology and Technique for further explanation.

Terminology and Technique / 103

Jumps, Leaps and Hops - Continued

Assemblé - (Jump) as in classical ballet meaning to bring together.

Double Attitude Grand Jeté - Like the Grand Jeté but both knees are bent, one in front attitude, one in back attitude. This is done moving in one direction or turning.

Frog Jump - Jump with feet in frog position. Legs are under the body in double passé turned out. Hands can be in varied positions.

Grand Jeté Leap Turn - This is done either with straight legs or with the back leg in an attitude. There is a two step turn in between the leaps.

Jumps, Leaps and Hops - Continued

Hitch Kick (like a temps de fleche) - This is a scissors like movement in which one leg passes by the other while in the air. It can be executed front or back.

Starting from passé   1

Starting with straight leg   2

3

4

5

6

7

Terminology and Technique / 105

Jumps, Leaps and Hops - Continued

Hurdlers' Leap - Like a jazz split in a leap. When executed correctly, this leap is both powerful and effective on the stage.

Variation: Lean forward toward the front leg.

Pike Jump - Legs are together and are extended in front of the body. Legs are kept straight and, ideally, they are parallel to the floor.

Prance (Leap) - Shift weight from one leg to the other to resemble a horse prancing. Knees are picked up while the feet are kept low. This can be done as a low prance with knees slightly lifted, or high prance with knees lifted higher off the floor.

Jumps, Leaps and Hops - Continued

Second Position
a. **Hop** - In 2nd position, hop on one leg keeping the other leg straight to the side or in attitude to the side.

Variations: 2nd position hops

Side layout

Top leg turned in, bottom leg passé

Top leg attitude, bottom leg straight

Top leg straight, bottom leg passé

Terminology and Technique / 107

Jumps, Leaps and Hops - Continued

Second Position
b. **Jump** - Russian. Also called a spread eagle or a toe touch.

Second Position
c. **Leap** - Like a grand glissade. This is performed to the side with body facing forward.

Sissonne - (Jump) as in classical ballet.

Split leap
a. **Grand Jeté** - With leg straight, brush through 1st position into leap onto same foot. Try to achieve a full split in mid air.

b. **Saut de Chat** (développé leap) - This is called the Jump of the Cat. It is like a grand jeté except the first leg développés to split position.

Terminology and Technique / 108

Jumps, Leaps and Hops - Continued

Stag
a. Jump - From two feet to two feet.
b. Hop - From one foot to same foot.
c. Leap - From one foot to the other foot.

Switch Leap
a. Battement - Straight leg brushes through 1st position.
b. Grand Pas De Cheval - Called the step of the horse. Enveloppé the leg (bring back) to passé and extend to arabesque.
c. Switch leap into 2nd position - This can be done from either a battement or a grand pas de cheval.
d. Start to corner and finish to front.
e. Grand Rond de Jambe - En l'air. Extending and carrying forward leg through 2nd position to arabesque while in the air.
f. Double Attitude - Through attitude front to attitude back or through attitude back to attitude front.

Tuck Jump - Both knees come up and are tucked to the chest. This type of jump is used in gymnastics.

General Terms - Continued

TURNS

See notes on Terminology and Technique for further explanations.

General Terms - Continued

PBS THEORY OF TURNS

PBS is what I refer to as the three components for a successful turn. Turns, whether simple, asymmetrical, or off balance, from classical ballet to funky jazz, have PBS in common.

> P...Placement
> B...Balance
> S...Spotting (focus)

The combination of the three (placement, balance, and spotting) allows for proper momentum, placement, and control to execute correct turns.

Placement and balance can be achieved in the classroom. Though the ability to spot is inherent, it, too, must be developed and strengthened in class. If one of the necessary components is missing, there must be compensation in one of the two remaining. For example, If there is inadequate spotting, there must be greater balance.

It is interesting to note here that not all turns are spotted. For example, in ice skating, if skaters spot, they interrupt the centrifugal force that is required for their spins. In dance, a turn without spotting is called a spin.

Turns - Continued

Attitude Turn - Leg is in attitude either front, side, or back. The turn may be inside or outside.

Barrel Turn (see terminology for explanation and photo)

Chaîné Turn (as in ballet) - In Jazz it may be performed in several ways. For example, it can be done in plié, plié relevé, 2nd position with no turnout, etc.

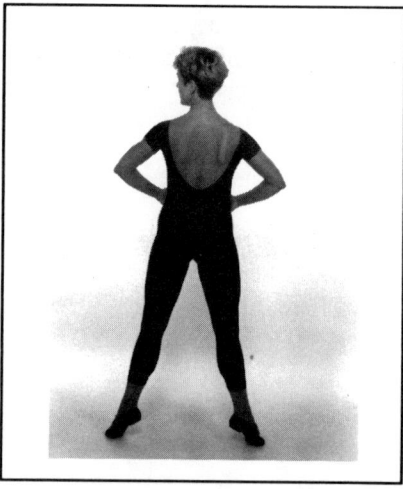

1

2

Turns - Continued

Compass Turn - Like an open arabesque. The working leg (foot) is close to the floor. This is normally executed as an inside turn.

Corkscrew Turn - Cross right leg over left, turn, step with left and turn. Accent with arms.

Arms can be:
   1. Right elbow to stomach, left arm extended (as if forming half of a "V.")

   2. Shampoo right arm.

Terminology and Technique / 113

Turns - Continued

First Arabesque Turn (as in ballet).

Inside Turn (jazz style: passé neutral) -Turn toward the supporting leg.

Turns - Continued

Jazz Pas de Bourrée Turns -

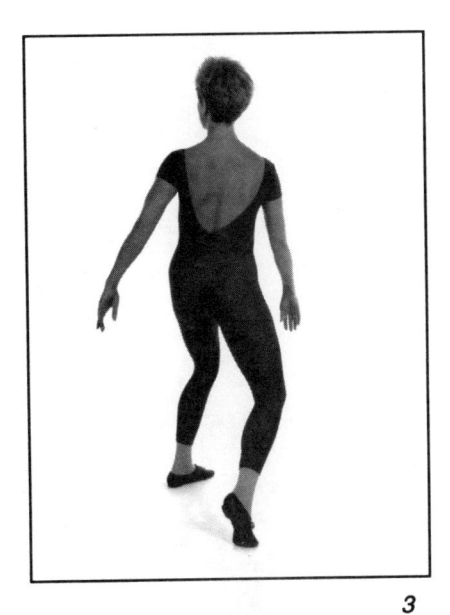

   a. Inside toward the supporting leg.

   b. Outside away from the supporting leg.

Terminology and Technique / 115

Turns - Continued

Outside Turn (jazz style: passé neutral) - Turn away from the supporting leg.

Paddle Turn (as in tap dance) - May be performed as an inside turn or an outside turn. A paddle turn has been described as a compass turn with ball changes.

Pencil Turn - Usually performed in neutral first. Turning on the ball of the foot, the other foot is lifted slightly off the floor. Toes can be either flexed or pointed. Legs remain straight.

Turns - Continued

Second Position Into Passé Turn - Leg is extended from body into second position then into passé either turned out or neutral.

Soutenu Turn (as in ballet) - In jazz dance, this can be a touch step turn, inside or outside.

Tap Step Turn - Outside or inside like a soutenu turn.

1

2

Terminology and Technique / 117

Turns - Continued

Three Step Turn - A full turn requiring three steps. Step side, step to face back, step to face front, step tap. For example: Step right to side, step left to face back, step right to face front, tap left to complete turn. Can begin to the left. A three step turn is used to travel and is generally performed as an inside turn.

1

2

3

4

Terminology and Technique / 118

CHAPTER 4

PLANNING A JAZZ DANCE CLASS

Whether you begin your class with standing exercises or floor exercises, the sequence of those exercises and movements is important.

THE BASIC SEQUENCE FOR ALL CLASSES IS:

STRETCH
WARM-UP
ISOLATE
STRENGTHEN
TONE
LARGER MOVEMENTS (including jumps, turns, and big combinations.)

Exercise

Here is an example of an exercise that begins standing, goes to the floor and returns to standing. It is for an intermediate to advanced class.

1

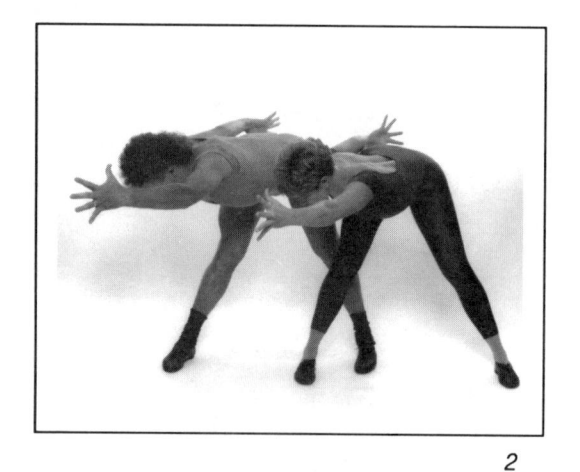

2

3

4

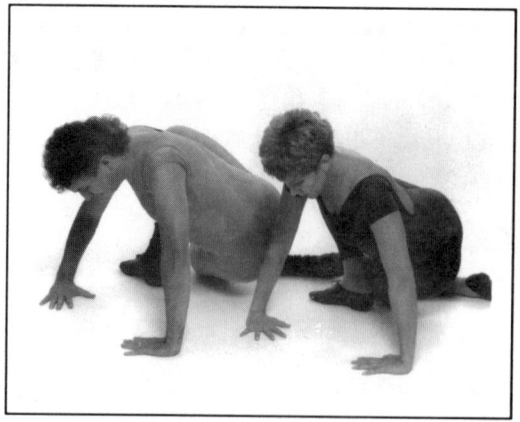

5

Exercise - Continued

6

7

8

9

10

11

Planning A Jazz Dance Class / 121

Exercise - Continued

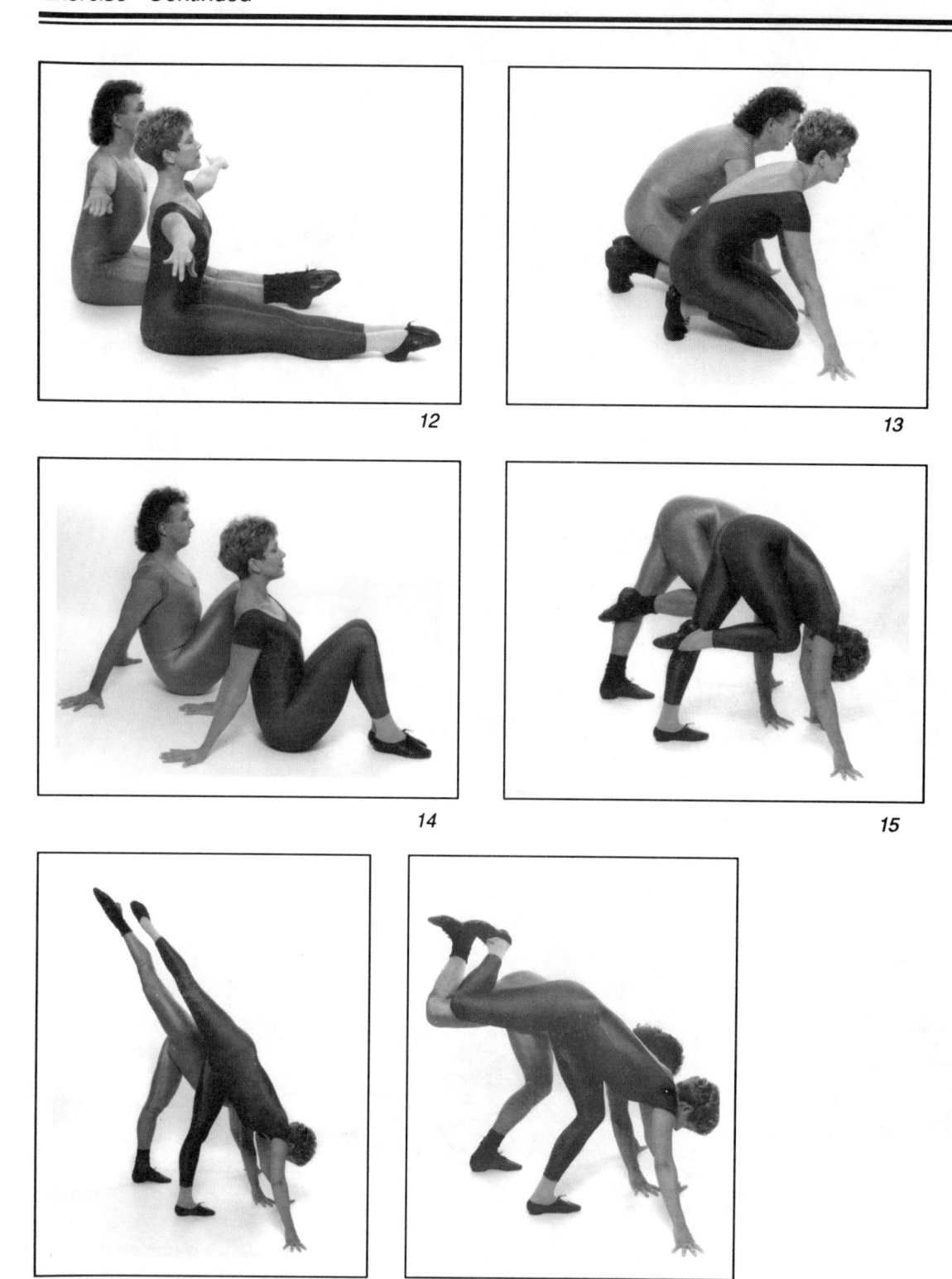

12

13

14

15

16

17

Planning A Jazz Dance Class / 122

Exercise - Continued

18

19

20

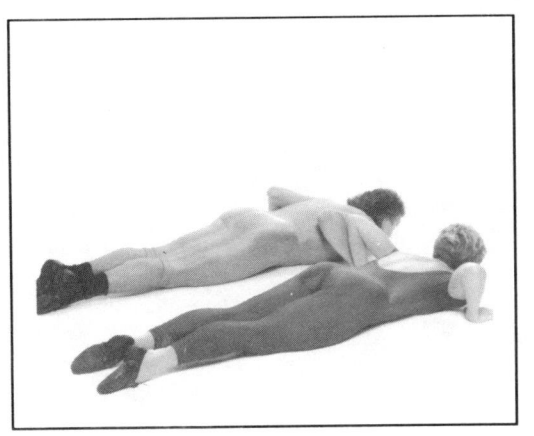

21

22

Planning A Jazz Dance Class / 123

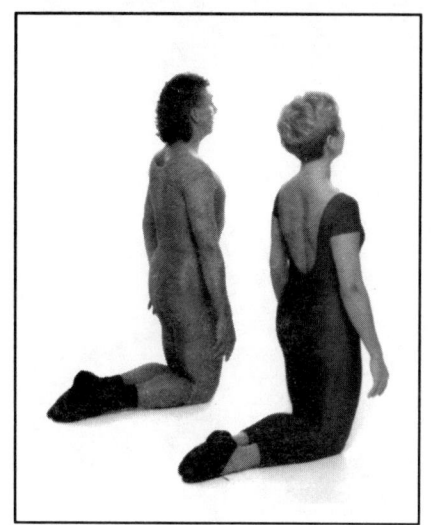

Exercise - Continued

23

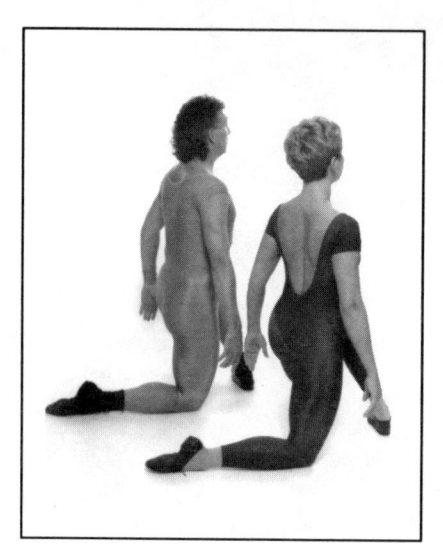

24

25

Planning A Jazz Dance Class / 124

Class #1

The following examples are for a 1 hour class. If the class is longer (many classes are 1 1/2 hours or more,) simply expand the time of each section discussed below.

CLASS #1: Begin With Standing Exercises

A. Stretch the major muscle groups first, combining them with isolations, pliés and footwork....15 to 20 minutes.

- With legs straight and feet in 2nd position parallel, round torso over and down. Head is relaxed. Roll up to beginning position.

- Keep legs and feet in 2nd position parallel and bend from the waist with a flat back. Arms are extended in a "V" with head in line with the spine. From a flat back with torso parallel to the floor, round the body over the legs. From either round or flat back, slowly roll up the body to standing.

    Note: I have indicated parallel position of the feet however, both of these exercises can be done in either parallel or turned out position.

Warm up and stretch in 1st, 2nd, 4th and 5th positions either parallel or turned out. (It is not common to exercise in 5th position parallel.) These exercises warm up the hamstrings and the lower back. Once they are warmed, dancing is easier and looks natural.

Isolation exercises must be done to warm up the part of the body that will be used in the class. For example, if you're using a combination that includes a head roll, you must warm up with head isolation exercises (such as head rolls.) The same applies to other parts of the body.

B. Floor stretch and strength....15 minutes. These are done sitting on the floor. Exercises for stretch and strength can be done in any position. I have included 1st and 2nd position exercises.

- First position with no turn out in which the legs are straight and directly in front of the body.

    Note: In a seated position, the maximum body weight is available for stretches.

- Exercises in second position with contractions and releases (arches) such as:

Class #1 - Exercises - Continued

Lying on back with right or left leg up

Lying on side with leg lifted

Lying on stomach and lifting legs alternately

2nd position turned out

2nd position on back stretching

For flexibility of the back and strength of the center, it is important to do exercises with arches as well as contractions. This centers the body and provides proper placement.

Note: proper placement is very important while doing the floor work. Refer to Plumb Line Method (p. 44)

Class #1 - Continued

Partner Stretches - Stretches for two people - used for intermediate and advanced classes. In addition to the physical benefit, partner stretches help to develop trust in fellow dancers. Partners should have the same leg length and, ideally, similar weight.

■ On the floor - Purpose: to strengthen and loosen back and backs of the legs. Also prepares for splits.

Planning A Jazz Dance Class / 127

Class #1 - Partner Stretches on the Floor - Continued

7

8

9

10

11

12

Planning A Jazz Dance Class / 128

Class #1 - Partner Stretches - Standing

■ **Standing - Purpose:** To strengthen and loosen backs and legs. This works on balance and uses the body weight and strength of partners to stretch.

Standing in 2nd position parallel, dancers are back to back approximately 6 inches from each other. Round over to floor, hold right hands through center of legs and pull. With left hand on partner's ankle, reach from outside. Place hands on floor and roll up. Relevé and balance. Place arms in 2nd. Place heels down and start again with left hands reaching. This exercise helps to prevent hyperextension of legs.

1

2

3

4

5

6

Class #1 - Partner Stretches - Standing - Continued

■ Standing - Purpose: To increase all degrees of back arches.

Note: These stretches can be adapted to needs of the individual partners however, if there is an injury, especially lower back or hamstring, the exercises should not be performed.

1

2

3

4

5

Planning A Jazz Dance Class / 130

Class #1 - Continued

C. Center Barre (standing)....10 minutes. When we refer to center barre exercises, we mean doing exercises in the center of the floor that are traditionally done at a barre (such as plié, tendu, etc..) Exercising at the barre develops balance. Exercising at center barre develops balance without support.

Use isolations and combine them with small movements that use little space. This can include movements that go to the sides, to the corners, and front and back or they might remain stationary. Example: jazz square, jazz walks, jazz pas de bourrée, and jazz pas de bourrée turns, pirouettes and fan kicks. (See classroom diagram.) If the level does not call for movement with isolation studies, you may omit them however, I recommend including either short or long isolation studies in your jazz class structure.

Often students are so anxious to "dance," they try to rush through exercises. This is a good time to explain the importance of floor work and other exercises. The more students know and understand about "why," the easier it will be for you, the teacher, to maintain their interest and energy levels during the more tedious stretches and warm ups. An educated teacher who imparts knowledge will be rewarded with excellent students who are both caring and devoted.

You should be aware of which exercises are suitable and appropriate for each class. For example: an adagio is fine for intermediate and advanced levels; I don't recommend chaîné turn head rolls with beginners and students under 11 years old.

Now that your class is stretched and warmed up, we can move on. In the next section, you will incorporate développés, battements, and turns.

D. Large Patterns....20 minutes. It's important to get the class up and moving after doing stationary floor exercises. It not only gets their circulation going but the activity also holds their interest. Large pattern exercises also help the students build self confidence while enabling them to pick up the choreography more easily. Work either in the center or diagonally from corner to corner. Use jazz pas de bourrées with turns, leaps and floor work including hitch kicks and switch leaps. Jazz runs and stylized exercises are good at this point. It's also a good idea to try to teach at least two different exercises from the corner or from side to side.

CLASS #2

A. Begin on floor....15 minutes. Though you can begin any class on the floor, this is more often the way to begin when the students are already warmed up from a class prior to this one (within the last hour or two.) These exercises are especially helpful during exam or performance weeks because stretching releases tensions and restores the reflexive quality that is often lacking when the muscles are tight or tired. When the muscles are tired, refrain from percussive pulsing. Studies show that good stretching results in better muscle conditioning which, in turn, results in fewer accidents and injuries.

> **Remember that exercises performed in a standing position are more easily adapted to individual bodies and limitations than those exercises performed in a seated position. For example, from a standing position, a student with a bad back can bend the knees to adjust the stretch.**

B. Standing....15 minutes. Make sure that isolations are done. If isolations are used in movements at center barre, in locomotive patterns, or combinations, those body parts will already be warmed up. Proper warm up will help prevent injury.

C. Placement Studies....5 minutes. Do turn studies at this time to work on balance. Good examples include pirouettes on one leg, turns in 2nd position, turns in attitude (both front and back), and off balance turns such as side layouts.

D. Across the Floor....10 minutes. Do at least two combinations including leaps, turns, slides, body rolls up and down to the floor, contractions to the floor, and back layouts that go the floor.

E. Combinations....15 minutes. Same as in Class #1.

Note: The final combinations should include movements or principles covered earlier in the class. Do not use movements that involve muscles or areas not properly warmed up.

THE CURRICULUM

Just as your classes are set up according to experience, ability, and maturity of the students, your curriculum for each class must also accommodate the differences.

Though it is possible to teach jazz to students with no prior dance training, I strongly recommend ballet for terminology, alignment, balance, strength and discipline. Modern Dance gives students the understanding of the floor work as well as the use of space and body weight. Tap gives the students a rhythm base from which to work and affords them the opportunity to understand syncopated rhythms and develop a personal style.

WHAT IS THE MINIMUM AGE FOR JAZZ STUDENTS?

There is so much controversy about when to begin teaching jazz that I feel I must address the issue here. I do not have formal jazz classes for students under nine years old. Of course, there are exceptions and occasionally, a younger student is physically and mentally ready for jazz.

There are ways, however, of getting around the "No jazz below age nine" policy and still keep the parents and students happy. You can give different names to the classes such as "Pre-jazz," "Novelty jazz," "Introduction to jazz," etc. I also incorporate some of the elements of jazz into other classes (tap and ballet).

If you are going to teach a "pre-jazz" class, it is suggested that you begin with barre work and introduce jazz isolations and steps that are "jazz in nature" such as jazz pas de bourrées, jazz squares, and Lindys. Proceed at a pace the students can handle comfortably. This class should be taught to students who are at least eight years old and who have prior training in tap and ballet.

Special care should be given to teaching jazz as such to students under nine years old. Their bodies: muscles, bones, and ligaments are not developed for certain moves we do in jazz, and as a result, students under nine are usually unable to execute the moves completely or correctly without causing injury. These moves include back layouts, hitch kicks and other techniques for which there must be maximum control of the lower back and legs. When teaching these younger students, avoid styles such as "Blues" and "Afro" and rhythms that incorporate Latin hips. Generally speaking, I do not recommend teaching hip isolations and exercises that over stretch because younger students are neither physically developed enough for the exercises nor emotionally developed enough for the mature styles.

LESSON PLANS FOR DIFFERENT LEVELS OF JAZZ

When we first start teaching jazz, classes are generally set up according to the students' ages. Ultimately, however, the students are separated into classes by ability and level.

NOTE: Remember: all classes begin with appropriate stretching and proper warm up.

▲ BEGINNERS JAZZ CLASS

1. Work on pliés and positions of arms and body in jazz dancing. (Refer to definitions.) When doing your warm up, be careful of hyperextension of elbows and knees.** Tendus and passés, both turned out and parallel, should be covered with much attention given to proper placement. Grand battement in all directions can be started at the barre.

** Note: Hyperextension is just that, over extension of the muscle. Do not lock the muscle but straighten it instead. To avoid hyperextension, the supporting muscles must be strengthened. For example, if the area behind the knee hyperextends, the thigh and calf muscles need to be strengthened. For a hyperextended elbow, strengthen the upper back and shoulder muscles. (A slight bend of the elbow eliminates the hyperextended look.)

2. Introduction to floor work for stretch and strength with exercises in the following positions:

   - Frog. Extend legs to 1st position and stretch over.
   - Side stretches in standing or seated 2nd position.
   - Bridges. Do easy bridge (release) exercises. Lie on back, legs in 1st position, hands in 2nd position with palms on the floor and shoulders down. Arch lower back up to sitting. Contract back down and repeat.

3. Basic locomotive steps and skills including walks, jazz walks, jazz runs, slides, small leaps, hops, and pivot turns.

4. Coordination exercises with simple locomotive (also called locomotor) patterns. In "The Art of Making Dance," Doris Humphrey (1958), includes the walk, run, leap, gallop, skip, jump, hop and slide as simple locomotive patterns. These are also the patterns that you will be using in your routines.

5. Simple turns, leaps, and hops.

Lesson Plans for Different Levels of Jazz - Continued

6. Introduction to lyrical jazz dance with simple port de bras and low développés.

7. Simple combinations. Symmetrical combinations (repeating the technique on the other side) are important to develop balance in both body and mind. Example: Start with right leg back,(no weight on right) step right to audience, pivot left, face back. Repeat step right, pivot left to face audience. Chassé right (no turn out) jazz pas de bourreé, turn left, kick ball change, forward right, outside turn right, land 2nd, passé neutral step left 2nd, step right 2nd and hold. Repeat entire combination beginning with left foot. Any comfortable, aesthetically pleasing arms can be used here.

▲ INTERMEDIATE JAZZ CLASS

Use same curriculum as beginning jazz class with the following additions:

1. Work on fast and percussive rhythms as well as the more difficult styles such as Blues and Lyrical.

2. Work on splits. This is important to open the hip sockets and increase the radius of stretch. Working on splits at this level results in nice leaps. It is not necessary to start with full splits. You may begin with jazz splits. (Open 4th on the floor. Ex: swastika).

3. Body roll and contraction. Begin standing or on the floor. If standing, legs are straight in parallel 2nd. Round upper body over to the floor. Plié and straighten as many repetitions as comfortable. Roll up and repeat. If on the floor, start in jazz split, straight leg, release over forward leg, contract up and repeat. Like a wave, release, contract. Remain up and stretch back leg to full split. Go through 2nd position, bend leg that was straight, face the opposite way and repeat exercise. Increasing the number of repetitions increases endurance.

4. Work on pelvis (hip) isolations.

5. Work on more difficult turns such as attitude turns. Work on multiple turns.

6. Emphasize working on change of level combinations that begin standing and transfer body weight to the floor and return to standing such as:

   a. From standing, split to floor and return to standing.
   b. Grand battement back layout, contract to floor and recover.
   c. Lunging right, fan kick left to crossed swastika to floor and stand.

Since there are many combinations within dances that change level and have floor work, these exercises are important to cover.

Lesson Plans for Different Levels of Jazz - Continued

7. Do combinations that are asymmetrical (one side only.) A good example is: kick right, step turn left, run left right, stag leap left, contract to floor. Because of staging, some combinations are asymmetrical and students should be able to perform them.

8. Work on building a quick mind by including combinations in single time, then in double time.

9. Have class perform large jumps, leaps, hops. Be creative with these moves and use different preparations to go into them.

▲ ADVANCED JAZZ CLASS

Same curriculum as intermediate and add the following:

1. Longer combinations. Do combinations for over 4 counts of 8.

2. Use difficult floor exercises that are used in an adagio. For example: start by sitting up in frog position. Développé right leg to 2nd, rond de jambe right leg back to attitude, place knee on floor, place left hand behind body and arch lower back, lift body toward ceiling, right arm up. Contract to swastika, left leg front.

3. Use partnering exercises. See Partner Stretches p.

4. Do multiple turns. Combine turns, leaps, jumps, hops. One of my favorites is: chaîné turn 4 counts beginning right, jazz pas de bourrée under, double or triple outside turn left, step left, run right, run left, développé, grand jeté right.

5. Work on leg extensions. Front, side and back. It is important to work on all layouts.

6. Encourage stylistic maturity. Polish details such as developing "musicality"...feeling the music.

7. Add improvisation into the class structure. Though this is optional, it is great fun and gives the students a chance to "choreograph."

8. Develop a well-rounded look both technically and with the required style. Technique alone is not enough. The attitude, the flair, the pizzaz are also important. This will help prepare the students for auditions and possible futures as performers, teachers and/or choreographers. It also gives the students poise and self confidence regardless of future endeavors.

▲ CHILDREN'S JAZZ CLASS

While we use many of the same elements in children's classes that we use in the beginner, intermediate, and sometimes advanced jazz classes, there are significant differences in teaching younger students. Use of appropriate music, ideas and attitudes is as important as understanding the level of physical maturity.

Children are easily frustrated and have limited concentration therefore, avoid difficult isolation studies, especially hip isolations. Children relate to Threatrical and West Coast styles while Blues, Latin, etc. are usually too mature for interpretation and performance.

Class structure is critical. Drill the basics until they are polished and effortlessly performed. Children like repetition and knowing what is coming next but their attention span is less than that of older students... keep your classes changing and keep them fun. Children will work harder when nurtured...when they feel your concern for them. Patience and caring are the keys to successful children's classes.

▲ TEEN JAZZ CLASS

Adhere closely to the class structure of barre, standing warm up, floor work, center barre, across the floor and combinations. When teenagers decide to take dance, they often choose the jazz class. For many, it is the first dance class they have had or possibly the first since they were six or seven years old. Teen classes can be difficult to work with if basics have not been covered therefore, give special attention to teaching technique and exercises. As with all students, when there is strong focus on technique, improvement is faster.

Teen classes love the rhythms of today's music. Current music maintains high interest and energy, however, it is also important to introduce the class to music we use in concert jazz.

▲ ADULT JAZZ CLASS

Adult jazz classes are very rewarding if taught carefully with special attention given to the age and level of maturity. This is the most difficult age group to hold onto for a long series of classes for several reasons. First, the majority of the students are in the class for exercise and fun. Second, being adults, they don't have the motivation their children have. They don't usually aspire to careers in dance. Third, they are self conscious about donning costumes and performing in the recital. They don't look at the class as a long term project but more a short term, exercise opportunity and tension reducing outlet. Fourth, adults see their classes as unnecessary luxuries in a tight economy. Where they will sacrifice to provide dance for their children, their own classes are among the first expenses cut.

Adult students are generally self conscious. I like to use humor to put them at ease however, it is important to treat these students with respect and always maintain a professional manner.

Coordination and technical exercises are the most difficult to teach adults. I prefer to ease into those two areas by adding terminology and limited numbers of exercises. The benefit of the knowledge and exercises is cumulative.

Basic techniques must be presented and reviewed over and over. Adults do not seem to learn as quickly as their younger counterparts but once they do, they dance better and want more challenges.

I try to encourage my adults not only to take the class but also to perform on occasions. This does not mean just performance in the recital but also participation in other performances throughout the year. Performing helps them build self-confidence, respect for the teacher, and better understanding of their children who dance.

Photo: Heike Wippermann

CHAPTER 5

IT'S SHOW TIME

TIPS FOR SUCCESSFUL CHOREOGRAPHY

Learning how to choreograph is much like learning to dance. One can study the "masters," read and re-read books and magazines, understand the fundamentals and technical aspects, but until you actually "get your feet wet," your education is unfinished. Choreography must be learned by doing. Trial and error are the most critical and often the most effective teachers. Until you have experienced the elation of watching a work come together, or the disappointment of seeing it fail, learning is incomplete.

The best choreographers are the ones who combine study with a constant striving to become well-rounded, open minded, and understanding. Choreographing is truly a special experience with immeasurable rewards. Watching a new (or old) work come to life...watching the work performed on stage as it was created in the mind's eye...this is the ultimate experience for the choreographer.

Tips For Successful Choreography - Continued

Here are some simple guidelines I find helpful when I choreograph for both general students and performance companies.

- Know your dancers. Be aware of their capabilities and make maximum use of them. Don't shoot over your dancers' heads or under utilize their talents. The choreography will surely suffer.
- In jazz dance, it is important to know the structure of your accompanying music. This will help make it appear that the music was written exclusively for your choreography. (See recommended music lists.)
- Use the stage to your best advantage. Be aware of the strong and weak areas of the stage and make them work for you. (See stage diagrams.)
- Though you want to vary your choreography, use canons* (rounds) and repeat key movements and themes. This helps to keep the audience interested, involved, and reluctant to see the work end.
- Develop your ideas early in the piece. Use the movements to support them.
- Learn and grow from each work you produce.
- Good choreographers cannot live in a vacuum. Be sensitive to the outside world - the changes, the new concepts and attitudes.
- Watch what other choreographers are doing. You can learn a great deal by watching their work. Use this increased knowledge to keep your choreography vital.

*A canon (round) is a musical term in which a set is repeated by the next group before the first group has completed the set. For example, group one starts on count 1, group two starts on count 3, group three starts on count 5. This is similar to the way the childhood song "Row, Row, Row Your Boat," is sung in canon.

STAGING

By understanding staging, the choreographer can add impact to the work, highlight the strengths, and minimize the weaknesses.

Though as the teacher you may need to have all of your students appear on the front line at some point in the performance, your knowledge of staging will benefit both you and your students. Place your weaker students in the weaker spots on the stage, likewise, the stronger students in the stronger spots. If the weaker students are in stronger areas, it will make these students look even weaker. Therefore, putting them in weaker areas doesn't demean the students but, in fact, makes them look better because it doesn't focus on their weaknesses.

The same is true for your choreography. Your strongest movements will look even more spectacular when they appear in the strong areas of the stage. You showcase your choreography in its best light when you rely on your creativity, your past experiences, and your own insight. For example, the element of surprise is used to best advantage when a Russian jump or similar move is performed stage center, the strongest area of the stage.

The image created by the choreography on the stage should be an accurate reflection of the work as it appears in your mind's eye. Understanding staging gives you a key to maximizing the impact of your work.

Staging - Continued

DIAGRAMS FOR USE IN STAGING DANCE IN THE CLASSROOM AND ON THE STAGE.

Stage

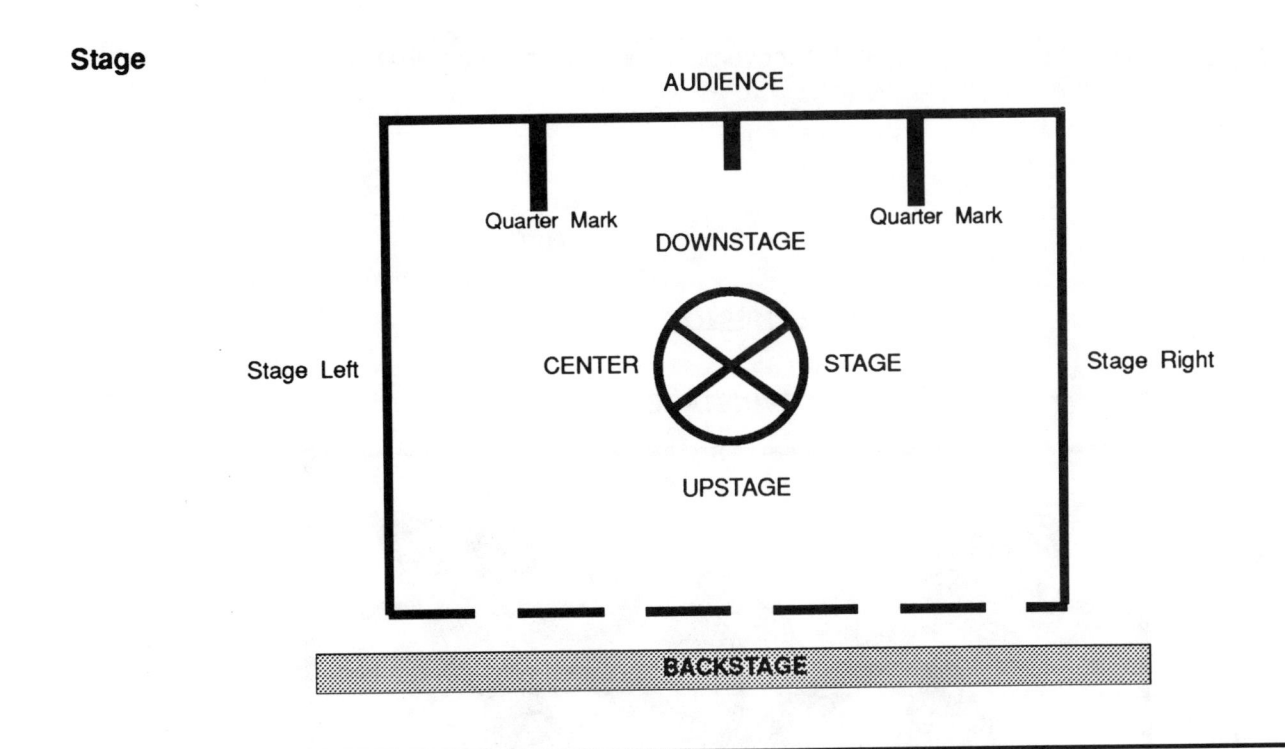

```
                        AUDIENCE
        ┌──────────┬───────┬──────────┐
        │          │       │          │
        │    Quarter Mark  Quarter Mark
        │         DOWNSTAGE           │
        │            ⊗                │
Stage Left    CENTER   STAGE    Stage Right
        │          UPSTAGE            │
        │                             │
        └─ ─ ─ ─ ─ ─ ─ ─ ─ ─ ─ ─ ─ ─ ─┘
                   BACKSTAGE
```

Class Room

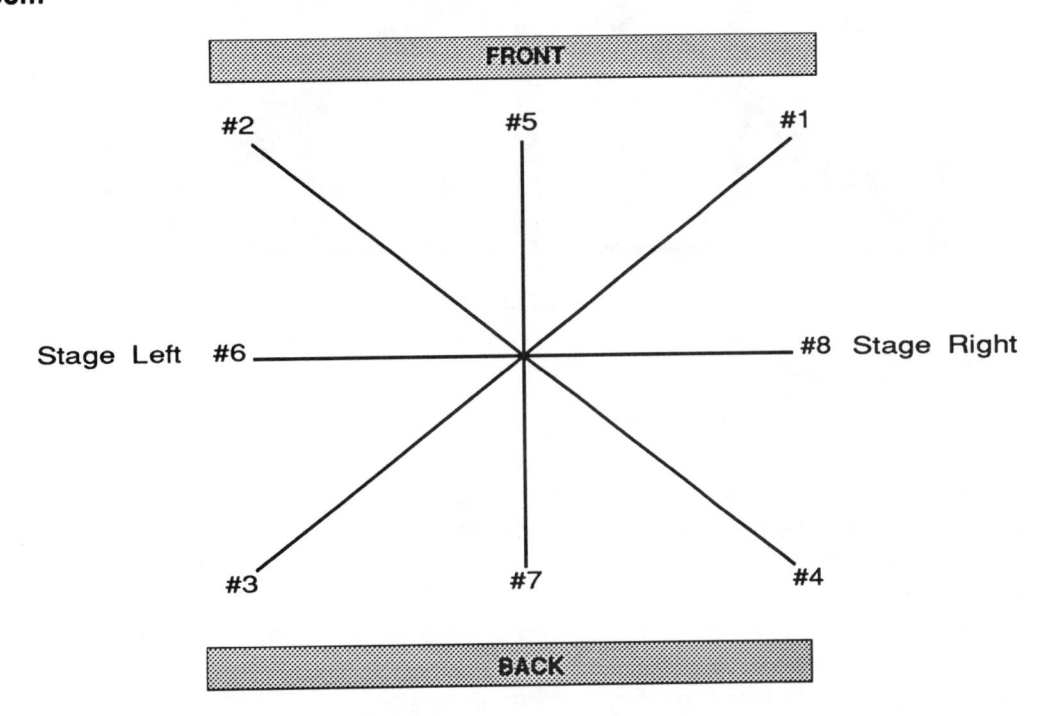

```
                    FRONT
        #2          #5          #1
          \         |         /
            \       |       /
              \     |     /
                \   |   /
Stage Left #6 ─────── ─────── #8 Stage Right
                /   |   \
              /     |     \
            /       |       \
          /         |         \
        #3          #7          #4
                    BACK
```

It's Show Time / 141

Staging - Continued

DIAGRAM OF THE STRONG LINES AND DIRECTIONS OF THOSE LINES CLASSROOM AND STAGE:

The bolder and wider the line, the stronger the movement and motion toward that direction.

AUDIENCE

DOWNSTAGE

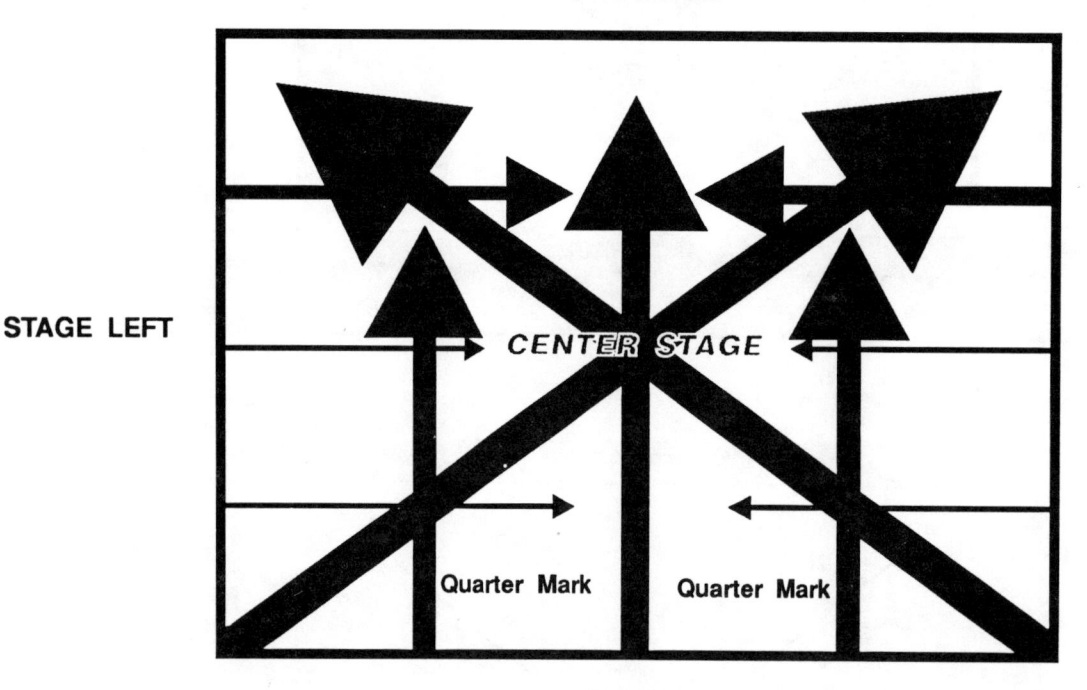

STAGE LEFT — CENTER STAGE — **STAGE RIGHT**

Quarter Mark   Quarter Mark

UPSTAGE

Strong lines are listed from the strongest to the weakest.
1. From corner upstage to the opposite corner downstage.
2. From upstage center through to downstage.
3. From stage right downstage moving to stage left.
4. From quarter marks (see stage diagram) upstage toward the quarter marks downstage.
5. From stage left downstage moving to stage right.
6. From stage right or left, directly through the center of the stage.

Staging - Continued

DIAGRAM OF THE STRONG AREAS OF THE CLASSROOM AND STAGE.

The larger the circle, the stronger the area. In other words, movement upstage becomes weaker while downstage, toward the audience is stronger.

AUDIENCE

DOWNSTAGE

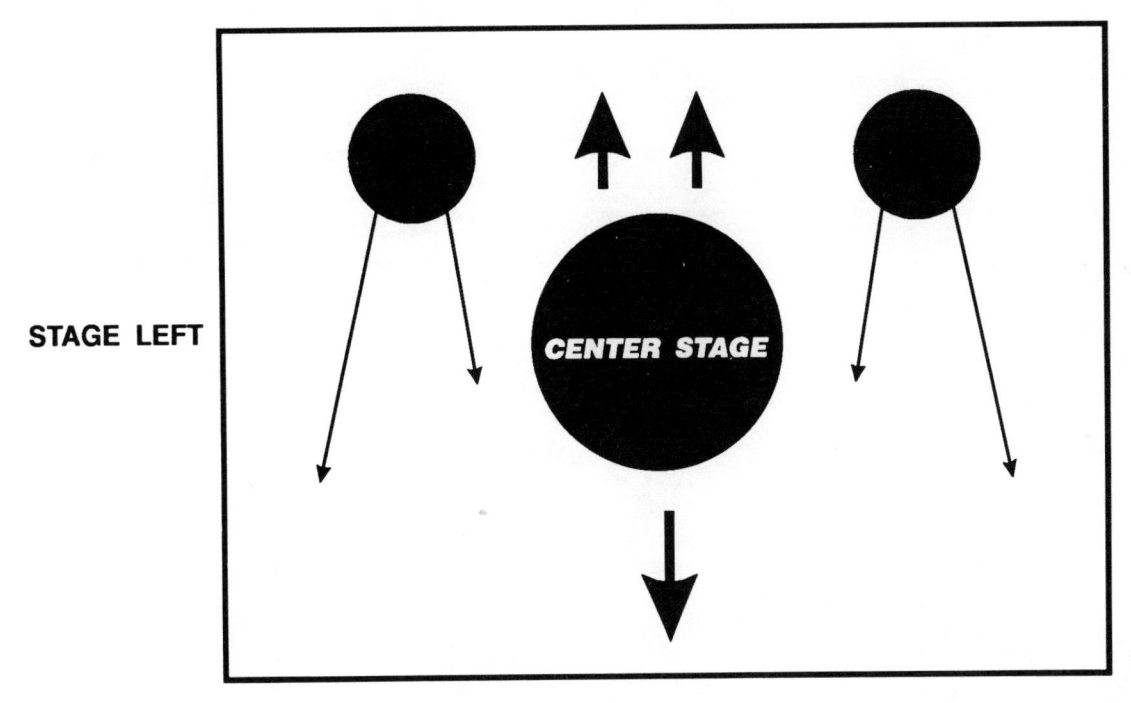

STAGE LEFT   **CENTER STAGE**   **STAGE RIGHT**

UPSTAGE

JAZZ DANCE TERMINOLOGY AND TECHNIQUE NOTATION

Knowledge of the origins and types of jazz, combined with the explanations, definitions and abbreviations I have included, will make the following dance studies and combinations easy to read and understand.

This system, including the style of notation, is a composite of ideas and theories gleaned from many of the teachers with whom I have studied and worked over the years. Because the following system is easy to interpret, understand and evaluate, it is very effective. It breaks down the counts (tempo) and the body movements. It also allows for explanations, in long hand, of difficult movements. The system is becoming so universally accepted that when teachers and teaching organizations have received notes, they have easily understood my directions and choreography.

The routines that are notated here include different styles, levels, and tempos and can be used as they are or broken down into sections. If questions should arise, remember to refer to the chapter on terminology and technique for assistance.

Abbreviations For Terminology & Techniques

Arabq . . . . Arabesque
Att . . . . Attitude
Aud . . . . Audience
Batt . . . . Battement
BC . . . . Ball change
Bck . . . . Back (place back or face back of audience or stage)
BLO . . . . Back Lay Out
BR . . . . Bridge
Ch . . . . Chassé (chase)
CHA . . . . Chaîné (turn)
CCC . . . . CHA-CHA-CHA
Cst . . . . Charleston Step
Cg . . . . Chug
Cpt . . . . Compass turn
Cont . . . . Contraction
Ct(s) . . . . Count(s)
Cr . . . . Cross
Dbl . . . . Double
Dev . . . . Développé
Diag . . . . Diagonal
Dig . . . . Dig
Dwn . . . . Down
Dg . . . . Drag
Ext . . . . Extend or extension
Fn Kck . . . . . . Fan Kick
FLO . . . . Front Lay Out
Frwd . . . . Forward
Frt . . . . Front (face forward)
Ft . . . . Foot
Fts . . . . Feet
Gd . . . . Grind
Gyr . . . . Gyration
Hd . . . . Head
Hnd(s) . . . . . . Hand(s)
HitKck . . . . . . Hitch Kick
Hp(s) . . . . Hip(s)
IS . . . . Inside
IST . . . . Inside Turn
J . . . . Jazz
JBug . . . . Jitterbug (as in movement)
JPDB . . . . Jazz Pas de Bourrée
JH . . . . Jazz Hand
JWP . . . . Jazz wrist press (also known as JRP)
Kck . . . . Kick
L . . . . Left
Ly . . . . Lindy (as in a style of jitterbug-like movement.)

Abbreviations For Terminology & Techniques - Continued

LOD	Line of Direction (direction/focus of movement)
Lg	Lunge
NTO	No turn out
Opp	Opposite
OST	Outside turn
P	Passé
Pdt	Paddle turn (as in tap dance)
Par	Parallel
Pelv	Pelvis
Plié	Plié (to bend)
Plié Rel	Plié Relevé
Pvt	Pivot
Pos	Position
1st	first position
2nd	second position
3rd	third position
4th	fourth position
5th	fifth position
R	Right
RC	Rib Cage
Rel	Relevé
Sham	Shampoo
Sh(s)	Shoulder(s)
Sk	Shake
Sl	Slide
SLO	Side Lay Out
Smmy	Shimmy
SOF	Sitting on Floor
Splt	Split
Sq	Square
Srt	Strut
St	Step
Stp	Stomp
Sut	Soutenu Turn
Sug Ft	Sugar Foot
Swat	Swaztika
Tm	Tempo (as in reference to timing)
Tp	Tap (as in foot action)
TO	Turn Out
TI	Turn In
Trn	Turn
Trp	Jazz Triplet
TT	Table Top
Twd	Toward
X's	Number of times something is performed (repetitions)
V	"V" position (arms and/or legs)
Wg	Wiggle
Wk(s)	Walk(s)

ROUTINES

This section includes choreography for beginners through advanced and gives you a good range of jazz routines.

▲ A Beginning Jazz Combination

RED HOT CHICAGO
Choreogaphy: Marcus R. Alford
Music: A medium tempo from a current artist including Janet Jackson, Paula Abdul, M.C. Hammer. etc.
Level: Beginner-Advanced beginner.

COUNTS	BODY MOVEMENTS	ARMS
START R FT FREE		
1-8	St R P NTO, Repeat L, Ch R JPDB Trn L	JWP R, JWP L, Dwn
1-8	Tp R St L Tp L St R, St Bck R, L, R, L	fist R, fist JH shake Hnds 2nd
1-8	Repeat above moving forward	
1-8	4th Pos L heel up, P TO R St R	V, Dwn, Sh roll, Dwn
1-8	Repeat above	
1-8	St L Tp R 2x, L cr Swat	Dwn
1-8	L leg Bck Swat, R, JH R to corner 3, sit spin R Swat corner 1, JH L corner 1	
1-16	JH R over chest, Swat Roll around floor, R Swat Roll around up to corner 1, cr R over L, stand open (R ft Free)	
1-8	St R St L, JPDB R, P L NTO	Dwn, snap on P
1-8	Repeat above L	
1-8	Assemblé ct 1, jump of choice ct 2, group walk to triangle	
1-4	St R St L, jump in 1st 2x, jump up to 2nd, Dbl fist 90°	R elbow up, L elbow
5-8	Repeat above 4 cts	
1-8	Repeat above 8 cts	
1-8	2nd Pos NTO, RC & Hd R,L,R,L P R St P L St	cr fist, V fist 2x
1-8	Repeat above first 6 cts, OST Trn L cts 7 & 8	
1-8	St R P L, St L P R, P L, P R, P R, Tp R, end open R ft free	JH R 2nd, JH L 2nd Repeat double time

It's Show Time / 147

Routines - Red Hot Chicago - Continued

COUNTS	BODY MOVEMENTS	ARMS
1-8	St R St L Trp RLR, repeat L (Traveling St)	JH R over R Sh, JH L over L Sh, repeat triple time
1-8	Repeat Above L	Repeat L
1-8	Kck BC R, P R St R NTO, JPDB L face corner 2, Batt R BLO (Optional)	JH R, JH L, JH R, Dwn
1-8	Hold cts 1,2, Tp L St L face Frt, St R St L Hop R NTO St R	JH 2nd, spiral, Dwn
1-8	St L P NTO R Hold, 3 St Trn R, Bck Att TO L, cr.	clap, Dbl fist Sham R on Trn, Baseball bat Pos on ct 8
1-8	(FLOOR WORK - ROUND OPTIONAL) Face side 8, knee hinge to floor, L Hnd up, JH ct 4, split R, cr, cts 5-8	
1-8	sit spin R, cts 1-4, face side 6 V Pos legs, JH 2nd arms, cr R over L, stand up.	
1-8	Reverse above L, (cr R over L to stand up)	
1-8	Tp R Frt,Bck,Frt,Bck,Ch R BC L R	cr JH, open JH, cr JH, open JH, Dwn
1-8	6 Wks in circle L, face side 6 JPDB under L cts 7 & 8	
1-8	R Knee BC, Kck R, JPDB L Trn St R face corner 4	JH 2nd, spiral on Kck
1-8	Face Corner 4, 2nd Pos. NTO Hnds Bck of Hd, contract, bent knees, arch up, Hd swing R, L, repeat	
1-48	Repeat Study L	

End

Routines - Continued

▲ A Beginner-Intermediate Funky Jazz Combination

EVERYBODY DANCE
Choreography: Marcus R. Alford
Music: " Everybody Dance Now" (Make You Sweat) by C.C. and the Music Factory.
Medium Tempo- Heavy Accents
Level: Beginner-Intermediate Jazz

COUNTS	BODY MOVEMENTS	ARMS
START	Face Bck 2nd NTO	Dwn
PART 1		
1-8	Accent Cts 1,3,5 different poses	
	face Frwd Ct 7, face Bck start Pos	
	2nd NTO spiral body R TI L leg 2nd	V JH up,wrap L over stomach
	NTO arch Bck recover,JPDB half Trn L	R in Bck, V JH up,clap
	Frt	over Hd,drop fist to Hps
1-8	Stp R,L,R,L,CCC,R,CCC L	fist Hps
1-8	Pvt side 6 Stp L,Pvt side 8 Stp L	fist Hps
	P R Hp lift Stp R,P L Hp lift Stp L	
1-8	Drop Hnds floor 2nd NTO Stag jump	touch floor,clap over Hd
	Stp RL leg Bck on floor TO R leg,	Dwn floor
	Body face floor L leg straight Bck	
1-8	Bend L leg NTO,TO R arms support body	
	Ct 1, hold Ct 2, rotate body to L side	
	R NTO bent, JH R on Ct 4 2nd, look Aud	
	Ct 6,Cr R over L Ct 7, stand up Ct 8	
POSES		
1-24	Pose every 4 Cts	
	(1.) Cr R over L JH corner 1 V low flat	
	Bck (2.) Stp L TI R leg, R JH up drop L	
	Dwn, look up (3.) Cr R over L JH 2nd R	
	L drop,look at Aud (4.)OST L NTO JH R	
	to chest, end 2nd face Aud (5.) reach up	
	R, look up 2nd NTO (6.) reach R leg Cr,	
	arms low V, corkscrew Trn L, Stp L	
	(When working in 3 or 4 lines, every	
	other line begins with pose 5 as the	
	1st pose, then in order of sequence)	
TRANSITION STEP		
	This movement will carry you to different	
	areas of the stage in different formations	
1-16	Cuban or Latin Wks,begin R Ft end L Ft	touch Hnds to Sh,wrist
		roll Dwn,touch Hnds to Sh
		V up, palms out, 8x

Routines - Everybody Dance - Continued

COUNTS	BODY MOVEMENTS	ARMS

PART 2

1-8 — 2nd NTO (funky) Sh R up, Sh L up, repeat flex R Att Tl to body 2x — no arms on Sh, JWP flex corner 1 on Att 2x

1-8 — Repeat above

1-8 — JPDB Trn, Batt R 2nd Stp R, Stp L open Stp R Cr, high 1st Arabq-slide, Stp R Cr — Dwn, L up R LJA, Dwn, L up R 2nd LJA, L JH Dwn

1-8 — Stp L Bck Stp R Bck, Rel TO 2nd, hold Ct 4, arch, Plié Tl support leg, Twd side 6 ct 5, recover to TO Rel, arch Plié Tl support leg, Twd side 8, recover to TO Rel — Dwn, 2nd fist, R wrap Frt, 2nd fist, L wrap Frt, 2nd fist

1-8 — Heels Dwn Ct 1, Tl legs CT 2, TO 1st Ct 3, Plié Hd release Ct 4, P R Tl Ct 5, Stp R Frwd, JPDB Trn L Cts 7&8 — Fist, JH, V JH, Table top JH Dwn

1-8 — Hops in place NTO, 1st 2x, 2nd lg R, repeat L, repeat Trn R, repeat Trn L (one group will Trn hops 2x, no Trn hops 2x) — Into body reach L Frwd, into body reach R Frwd, repeat

1-8 — 2nd NTO, RC up, lower Bck release 4x (funky) repeat L, repeat 3x — R Palm over, R Sh, L Dwn,

1-16 — — Repeat above 16 Cts

TRANSITION STEP

1-16 — Travel to different area of stage into a new formation, suggested 2 lines V with point up stage

PART 3

1-8 — Stp R Tp L, Bck Stp L Tp R Bck, repeat look R, look L, repeat — JWP L Cr, JWP R Cr repeat

1-8 — 3 Pas de chats NTO to R, Stp R, L look R, L — Dwn

1-8 — Jump R over Cr 4th, open 2nd NTO 2x, relax 2nd Stp R Bck Stp L Bck, chug to side 6 face side 8, release Bck & Hd Ct 8 — Cr JWP Flex, open JWP Flex drop, R Hnd R Sh, L Hnd L SH, drop

1-8 — Repeat above L

1-8 — Stp R Att Tl L low, Stp L Att Tl R low Stp R Tp L, Stp L Tp R 2x Stp R low Att TO Trn(hop)R JPDB L under, 4 small low Pas de chats R, Frt, R, R side R, Bck L, L side — R fist Diag, R elbow pull in repeat L, repeat 4x on beat Dwn, relax, fun

1-8 — Repeat above

It's Show Time / 150

Routines - Everybody Dance - Continued

COUNTS	BODY MOVEMENTS	ARMS
1-8	Kck R Att flex Ft Frwd Stp R,pencil Trn L 2x OST,CHA Trn in place L,look R,look L	JWP 4th L,JWP Twd floor low R palm R Sh,L palm L Sh
1-8	fall to floor 2 Cts in push-up Pos Frwd,Trn to L 1x,knee to floor Ct 5, tuck 2nd TI slightly off floor Ct 6,look Frwd,repeat Ct 5,hold Ct 8	push-up L up,R up,support body on floor
1-8	Stp R Frwd TO,JPDB Trn L standing L Stp R Ft Bck,L Ft Bck,Tp R TI hold Ct 8	JH over Hd,R JH 2nd,Dwn palm over R eye,face Frwd,or Dwn
1-8	J Sq R over L,Pvt corner 4 R Stp corner 2 L,Pvt corner 2 R Stp Frwd L,Hd swing R,L,Sh roll R,L,Sham R,L P NTO R,Stp R, Ch L,R knee on floor, Cr Swat,Bck roll,end tuck face corner 4	Clap Frt body,JH Diag,R up with JH L in Frt of chest R fist rolls L through JH support body with arms
1-8	(In canon) on knees body corner 4 look to Aud	JH Diag L 2nd
1-8	J split 2nd R Cts 1-4,relax R Ct 5,low flat Bck look corner 1 Ct 6 hold Cts 7&8	L up JH,R 2nd,on J split, Hnds slap floor beside Ft Ct 5
1-8	seat spin Bck Twd R Cts 1-4,end 2nd TO bent knee body lifted,look R Ct 7 look L Ct 8	push floor to spin
1-8	Clap Hnds over Hd,straight leg Ct 1 look up Ct 2,look to Bck Ct 3 drop Hnds Frt of body Ct 4,split R L arm up,face Aud	
1-8	Bring L leg over,face side 6,on stomach hold Ct 3, JHs reach side 6,look side 6 flex,Ft Ct 4,push Bck to NTO 1st body over	
1-8	P L NTO,Stp L Frwd,TI 1st,hold Ct 4,TO 1st,TI 1st 2x,travel to R	Clap Hnds Frt chest,place R Hnd Frwd,L Sh,R JH to floor JWP Flex R&L

<u>TRANSITION STEP</u>

1-16   Travel to beginning positions
        Repeat beginning pose,end face Bck
          **Suggestion: Choreograph poses in pairs or trios.

End

Routines - Continued

▲ A Blues Adage

DR FEELGOOD
Choreography: Marcus R. Alford
Music: "Dr. Feelgood" by Aretha Franklin or may be performed to "Dr. Feelgood" on the album, "Live in Paris" by Dee Dee Bridgewater
Level: Intermediate-Advanced
Adagio Jazz Dance

COUNTS	BODY MOVEMENTS	ARMS
1-8	St R St L Batt R cross,St R JPDB L w/head roll P R NTO	Dwn,2nd Pos,V, R,2nd L, cr
1-8	St R lg R NTO, R Bck,sit	V,pos. JH, Dwn floor,R JH Aud
1-8	fan kck R L,stand face Bck,Hp roll L, P NTO L,Tp L	Dwn, R 2nd R drop over Hd.
1-8	Hp roll L 3x (traveling),on ct 7,8 spiral to frt	R slow drop, 2nd pos, bent elbows on 7
1-8	Batt 2nd cr R over L,P L,Hps L,R,L,St L	2nd JH over Sh R up JH,L up R up
1-8	OST Att Trn R,P NTO ct 5,lg R leg Bck TO ct 7,8	2nd hug,stay
1-8	Body roll R to L,look Aud ct 4,IST L NTO, Batt BLO Frwd,lg R ct 8	hug, V,Dwn
1-8	stand,Wk Bck LRL, open 4th NTO,hold ct 7,8	V,pos,relax low 1st
1-8	knee hinge 4 cts Twd R, ST L Ft ct 5 touch R toe into L ft ct 5-8, NTO	R up,& Dwn 2nd palm Dwn, Drop Dwn,isolate L Sh ct 7,8
1-8	St R over L P NTO R St R,spiral SLO, Trn IST, NTO L Tp R Ft	R Dwn,up diag to half V, R cr Chest, R up diag to half V L 2nd
1-8	REPEAT above 1-8	
1-8	(IS DONE DOUBLE TIME) BC R cr R, BC L cr L, Kck BC R,OST R,soutenu Trn R,Cpt R, P L St L	Dwn,4th, in high 1st Arabq R fist R Hp, JH R low
1-8	St R St L St R St L JPDB R,Tp L, Sh roll on JPDB,7&, arch Bck ct 8	JH R JH L cr R over body,cr L over body JH up,2nd
1-8	P NTO L 4cts Cont on ct4,arch Bck 5-8, St L TO	up slow,scoop Bck to low V cts 6-8
1-8	St R to Corner #3 St L St R P L w/cont arch Bck 6-8	Dwn,up,scoop V

Routines - Dr. Feelgood - Continued

COUNTS	BODY MOVEMENTS	ARMS
1-12	(REPEAT TOTAL STEP 3X) St R,L,Trn Twd Aud,Fan Kck bent R knee NTO,Cont.	L up V,L 90°
12-16	Cont to floor roll R,arch release Hd face wall 6	Dwn
1-8	Cont over ct 1&2,roll up ct 3,4 face Bck St RLRL	R shape of Bk L reach Twd side 6

PART II
(Can be separate Adagio)

1-8	R arm up 1-4 cts. roll Hps L arm sham across Hd arch Bck 5,6 recover w/arm 7,8	
1-4	St L face Frt R Att open St Bck R, St Bck L St Bck R Tp L	R up V, L 2nd R circle Frt body reaches Bck on 4 L Dwn
5-8	St L,R,into 4th pos TO,Dbl OST ct 7 St L ct 8	4th pos,in
1-8	reach corner 4,R arm St R Ch corner 2 NTO, ct 2&3 Batt R leg corner 2 on ct 4 (Fouetté) to Frt R leg hold ct 6, plié Arbq.	
1-8	St Piqué R SLO L knee into body Cont ct 8, reach up JH V on SLO make fist over Sh on Cont	
1-8	chest dive croisé 1-4 ct, hands on floor, walk body Bck to legs cts 5-8	
1-8	Rond de jambe R leg to side 6,BLO ct 6 to floor cts 7&8	
1-8	R Hnd up JH cts 1-4 to ceiling,arch L knee on floor R knee up, on cts 5-8 place R knee Dwn increase arch	
1-8	fall to floor slowly to Aud ct 1,2, Rond de jambe R leg corner 2 cts 3,4 LO cts 5,6,arch up cts 7,8 (L knee bent)	
1-8	roll R corner 1 to corner 3	
1-8	come up open R leg Frt, L leg TO under (hold ct 2-4) sway cts 5-8, R Bck L, R Bck L.	
1-8	stand up R Frt cts 1-6 arms Dwn, St L ct 7, St R ct 8 St L Batt R,arms swing L to R,St R St L IST Att toe drag, R arm up L arm Dwn, St R P L NTO, reach R arm corner 4	
1-8	Push body to floor cts 1-4, release 1st Pos NTO Roll up cts 5-8	
1-8	Roll Frwd, end Swat R,ct 3,4, Hnds behind body, small arch, Dev R to corner 1 cts 5-8	
1-8	Lie w/weight on R Hp cts 1,2,L knee bent face Bck cts 3,4, Hnds floor, push/slide Bck, look R hnd, Relax.	

End

It's Show Time / 153

Routines - Continued

▲ A Hot Combination

WAR DANCE
Choreography: Marcus R. Alford
Music Edwin Starr's "War" or Bruce Springsteen's "War"
Level: Intermediate-Advanced Jazz

COUNTS	BODY MOVEMENTS	ARMS
PART 1		
START 2nd NTO Plié Cont		Dwn low 2nd
1-8J	tuck jump to Par 2nd NTO,hold ct 2 RC R,3L,4,PT I R,5 Stp R 6,P L NTO Stp 8	fist 2nd,elbows bent,cr J frame fist,JH floor
1-8	Stp R 2nd,Stp L 2nd,Ch R,Cha Trn L 2x coupe R Bck(Hd swing R,L Hd roll R)	JH,comb R,JH,comb L,JHs side Hd,JHs V,8
1-8	Stp R Batt L corner 4,JPDB Trn L,Batt R corner 1,JPDB Trn R	reach JHs corner 4,drop reach JHs corner 1,drop
1-8	travel side 8, Trp L,R,L,Stp R 2nd NTO face Frt,Stp L 2nd NTO face Frt	V,wrap L Frt,Repeat R,L fist 2nd R LJA,fist L LJA
1-8	Ch R,face Frwd,Stp L Cr Stp R, Barrel Trn in air,Stp L cr,Stp R open	LJA,L Dwn,R up airplane on barrel Trn,4th
1-8	Repeat 1-8 L	
1-8	Travel R circle Trp R,L,R,Stp L 2nd NTO,Stp R 2nd NTO	V,wrap R Frt,repeat L,R LJA fist L,LJA fist R
1-8	Repeat cts 1-7 from beginning on L Ct 8 Tp R Ft Bck,look Dwn	
PART 2		
1-8	BC R Bck,P TO R,BC Frt travel side 8 R FT Frt,Kck L low 2nd TO,Cr L over R, Stp R 2nd NTO	L up in half V,R up in half V,2nd spiral
1-8	OST L NTO,IST L end face corner 3 Ch R,Stag hop L Att R under,Stp L Tp R Bck	Round 2x,drop,V up,drop
1-8	corner 1 Ch R,corner 2 Trp L,leap R straight L Att from Bck,Twd Frt Stp L Plié Rel,P TI R hold Ct 8	4th 2x,L up R 2nd,JHs low V
1-8	CCC,R,L,BC Frt Tp R Bck,Smmy Hd Ct 7 look corner 1 ct 8	JHs low,Sh R,L,R,repeat L,drop
1-8	P NTO R,BC 2x side,repeat L,P TI R Cont,Plié L	reach corner 1,corner 4 JHs reach corner 4 Ct 7
1-16	Repeat above 16 cts	

Routines - War Dance - Continued

COUNTS	BODY MOVEMENTS	ARMS
1-8	Tp R Bck,Dbl P jump bring R Ft Frwd	wrist together, Hnds cupped at chin
	end 4th,jump up,to floor,Stp R Ft Frt Pt L Ft Bck Low Lg	look corner 1,look Frwd, Bck to Bck Hnds Dwn,R up in half V L on floor,look up R
1-16	sit face side 6,R Cr Swat,R NTO table top,L P on floor NTO,look Frwd Ct 4,flex Fts Ct 4,Stp R Dev L to ceiling Cts 1-4,Plié NTO L,Stp L hold look up	on floor,R palm Frwd LJA,L bent palm Bck,JHs Ct 4 floor,fist Hps,JHs V to side 6,JHs in Ct 8

PART 3

COUNTS	BODY MOVEMENTS	ARMS
1-8	2nd TO R,TI R,TO R,R Bck Lg L look up	LJA 2nd R,LJA JH R,2nd R,JHs Bck Twd R leg
1-8	P NTO R,OST R slow NTO	fist LJA 2nd Cr Frt chest fist,repeat
1-8	Ch R,Trp L,Wk R,L,R,L in L circle end 2nd	fist LJA spiral,drop R pull Bck,pull Frt 2x
1-8	Hd cont,Hd tilt R,circle Hd look Frt R,R Sh up,RC R Plié R JPDB L,Look up ct 8	on RC bend arm R elbow out,JH circle Twd body JH Dwn on JPDB
1-8	P TI R,Stp R Fwd Trp L half Trn,Stag leap R Frwd,Stp R Plié L leg Bck,FLO	R Hp fist,JWP Frwd,V, wrap R over L,V,Dwn reach corner 1 LJA
1-8	Batt L BLO,Stp L,Stp R P TO L Stp L, P TO R Stp R TO 2nd,Tp L Bck,look over R Sh	high 5th,V,R fist circle Frt body JH 2nd,repeat L reach JH 2nd L,drop L, reach R Dwn Twd L Ft

PART 4

COUNTS	BODY MOVEMENTS	ARMS
1-8	run to corner 1 R,L,stomach slide Cont Bck on heels (on Ct 5)	on floor,Bck V,push Bck
1-8	JH reach corner 1,Hd up Ct 2,diving push-up to floor Ct 3-4,stand up L Cts 5-8	
1-8	JPDB R,JPDB L Trn,Pvt R to Bck,Pvt R to Frt	2nd,wrap L Frt,Sham R,JH Dwn,slice LJA 2x on Pvts
1-8	1 OST R NTO,Dbl IST NTO,TP L 2nd BLO Cts 5-8	round,Dwn 2nd,accent JH BLO Ct 8
1-16	Repeat above last 16 Cts,start L	

Optional

COUNTS	BODY MOVEMENTS	ARMS
	Plié 1st NTO jump Stp R,Stp L,JPDB R, OST L	Dwn,JH up 5th,chest spiral 2nd R,repeat L,4th fist
1-8	continue OST Stp L Bck Att R,Lg,R corner 1,Cr Swat to corner 3	fist chest,JH R reach corner 1,L Hp L,Hnds Floor

Routines - War Dance - Continued

COUNTS	BODY MOVEMENTS	ARMS
1-8	Hd swing R,L,snap R,L,2nd bent elbow, place Hnds floor,Dev R 2nd,Dev L 2nd Stp L Lg Frwd side 8	
1-8	Stand up on L slow Cts 1-4,look at side 8, L Hnd L knee on Cts 5-7,R Hnd JH flat reach from side 1,look Frwd Ct 8 place L Hnd R Hp,release Hps	
1-8	Stp R Tp L, Stp L Tp R,Stp R in place Stp L in place,Stp R Tp L beside R	reach R Frt JH,fist R R Hp reach L up JH,pull L fist over L Sh,swing Hd R,L, Cr JHs Frt chest,JWP Frwd
1-8	Repeat above on L	

<u>Ending</u> Jump up crash to floor

End

It's Show Time / 156

Routines - Continued

▲ A Fast Hot Combination
TRANCE DANCE

CHOREOGRAPHY: Marcus R. Alford
MUSIC: Funky. Medium Tempo. "Trance Dance" from the album " A Little Bit of This, A Litle Bit of That" by D. Mob
LEVEL: Intermediate-Advanced Jazz

COUNTS	BODY MOVEMENTS	ARMS
(1st SECTION IN ROUNDS)		
PART 1		
1-8	(2nd NTO,START Pos.) JPDB R,L,R,L	R L JH 2nd "S" curve RLRL
1-16	St to corner 2 R,L,OST Trn 2 3/4, end Frt	point R index finger corner 2 on ct 2,Frt Trn,end spiral 2nd
1-16	Repeat Above L,(ROUND OVER)	
1-12	Repeat R (All Together)	
12-16	leap R 2nd,L cr Bck roll onto Bck on floor,end 2nd Pos,face ceiling.	LJAs 2nd,JWP R
1-8	Split L,face Aud,stand up St L,hold	
PART 2		
1-8	TRP in place R,L,spiral Trn 2x R	R reverse,Sham,LJA
1-8	leap R corner 1,St L Ch corner 3 R,Trn NTO,end Frwd St L St R	4th Pos JWP flex,2nd,Trn Dwn
1-8	Kck L corner 4,St L St R,P NTO L, St Bck L Tp R,hold,Smmy Hd cts 7&8	4th,flex R, fist to Hps,90 R JHs
1-8	St R St L CCC R,(side),St L cr R St L P NTO R	Dwn,up,dwn LJA Diag up
1-16	St R Tp L (sliding) St L Tp R 2x, St R Tp L St L,R,St L cr R,St L P NTO R,hold cts 15 & 16	free,JH,Diag R,up ct 7
PART 3		
1-8	Ch Bck R,Tp St Trn Bck(face Bck), Ch Bck R,Tp St Trn Bck (face Frt)	2nd,JWP on Ch
1-8	R slow cr L,L slow cr,R fast cr,L fast cr 2x	Sham.L,R, LRLR
1-8	cr R over L slow,cr L over R slow, St R Bck,Att Bck L,St L over R,Bck Att R,Plié L	2nd JH L,R R Hnd L Sh L Hnd R Sh JWP 4th L
1-8	R Pvt ST BC R,L,Pvt corner 2 R,L, St R over L Sug Ft LRL	Free

It's Show Time / 157

Routines - Trance Dance - Continued

COUNTS	BODY MOVEMENTS	ARMS
1-8	St R cr L over R St R Tp L,St L St R Bck,3 hops to face side 6, At NTO,cr L over R	fist R,JH R, 2nd,reverse, JWP ct 8
1-8	Jump 2nd NTO,cr L over R Jump, Jump 2nd 2x,Pvt R 2x face Bck,Frt	Free
1-16	Repeat Above 1-16	
1-8	St R St L,CCC (side) R,St L IST NTO L,CCC (side) R	elbows up,Dwn up,Dwn,up with fist,Trn arms cr
1-8	Reverse Above L	
1-8	Kck BC R over L,St R coupé Trn L TO St L St R Tp L beside R,Hd release ct 6 look Aud ct 7,hold ct 8	Hnd Diag R, bent in Trn,JWP R L Hnd on Bck
1-8	St L NTO 2nd Pos, R ft Bck Dwn, floor Lg L	
1-8	St L NTO 2nd Pos,R ft Bck Dwn,floor Lg L	
1-8	lie on floor L leg bent,Trn to L knees together,arms over leg,drop Hd to knee, hold cts 7,8.	
1-8	get up off floor any way you can (Please look good)	

(split dancers into 2 groups;STAGE R, has L ft free, STAGE L,has R ft free.)

1-32	BC Kck Lg,Ch Bck,stag leap,St Tp, release Hps,OST NTO cts 5,6,7,8, Repeat other side.	

End

Routines - Continued

▲ A Musical Theatre-like Combination

MORE
CHOREOGRAPHY: Marcus R. Alford
MUSIC: Song "More" from the album " Breathless" by Madonna
LEVEL: Intermediate-Advanced Jazz Musical
High Energy

COUNTS	BODY MOVEMENTS	ARMS
BEGIN	1st Par body rounded over,face Frt knees bent	Relax
PART 1		
1-8	Bounce Dbl time,rise to 1st Par	
1-8	R Ft sugar,out-in 3x,legs together Ct 8 Hd look R	Relax elbows,2nd
1-8	Cuban Wk Twd R	L Hnd L Hp,R Hnd touch L Sh R Sh,L ear,forehead,Hnd Dwn center on odd Cts,relax wrist
1-8	Repeat 2nd 8Cts of PART 1	
1-4	R Ft Twd Aud,Stp 2x,Stp JPDB face Bck	JWP,drop on JPDB
5-8	Repeat Cts 1-4,face Bck end face Frt	
1-8	Shuffle R leg,make movement large to side, Cr to Frt Twd L,BC 5x,Stp out L Ct 8	L up,R Diag Dwn
(Music has a pause)		
1-8	Balance R,L,Soutenu Trn R,Stp R look R	R up,L up,L Hnd Hp,JWP R
1-8	Repeat L	Dbl JWP
BREAK STEP		
1-8	Optional,Dbl or Triple time Step or Stp 4x,begin R	
PART 2		
1-8	R TI,TO 2x Par 1st,Stp R Flex L,Stp L Flex R	JH up body,low 5th, relax
1-8	Repeat	
1-8	Lg R IST R Dbl,Ch L,BC R,L Bck Cts 7,8	wrap R over L,on BC,limp wrist R
1-8	Stp R,Cr L Frt,2nd leap R,Tp L Ft Bck,flex L Ft side,Stp R Trp L in a circle	relax,2nd JH Bck,flex R Cr body Dwn,relax
1-32	Repeat PART 2	
PART 3		
1-8	Stp R Frwd TO,IST,Ch L open,Pelv Cont,release	wrap R Frt,L Bck at waist, fist,flex Hnds limp wrist

Routines - More - Continued

COUNTS	BODY MOVEMENTS	ARMS
1-8	Pelv Cont,release 2x,Sh 2x,P L TO. Rel R,Stp L 2nd,hold	flex-limp 2x,limp,Sh roll 2x,R up L Dwn,relax
1-8	Repeat last 1-8 Cts	
1-16	Ch JPDB corner 1,Ch JPDP corner 4 R,L,R,L,end open face Bck	low V Dwn 3x,Cts 15-16 JH R,L
1-8	face side 6,Stp R Ft look R,Stp L Ft look L,Stp R,L,R,L,Frwd look R,L,R,L,Frwd	Relax
1-8	circle R,Cpt 4x end face Frt	R up Cr Frt body 4x
1-8	Stp R,hold Ct2,Stp L,hold Ct4,Stp R,L,R,L,	elbow punch R-L,R,L,R,L,
1-8	CHA Trn R,CHA Trn L,end 2nd,plie'	fist touch Sh,V,fist touch Sh,R Hnd floor,L Hnd up
1-8	Barrel Trn R leg,R toe Bck,slide to chest,on floor,face Dwn	windmill R,L,push to floor Hnd under Sh Ct 7,hold Ct 8
1-2	(Floor work) small arch,bend R knee Ft should be seen,hold Ct 2	push against floor
3-4	Trn R face Bck,sit up L leg 2nd,R Ft floor L Hnd Bck of body	
5-8	arch (in a canon) up,Rel R Ft	
1-2	Bring R across and under L leg,sit in Swat R in Frt	
3-6	Stand face corner R,R Ft Bck	
7-8	Half Trn Tp L Bck,Sh roll Ct 7, hold Ct 8	

PART 4

COUNTS	BODY MOVEMENTS	ARMS
1-8	2nd Tp L Ft,Hp roll L Cts 1-2,Stp L,R,Twd corner 2,Att L Rel R,arch Bck,Stp L.R	Dwn,R Cr 2nd,R up & Bck Dwn
1-8	Hp lift Par,Stag leap R,R Ft Tp 2x Stp JPDB L Trn	Dwn,circle scoop R,L, relax R Hnd Cr body L Hnd V,Cr Bck
1-8	Rond de jambe J Wks Frwd 4x	R wrap,L V
1-4	Ch R coupé Dev L SLO	R 2nd L Hnd at R Sh
4-8	Stp L Stp R Cr L,Stag hop R bck	relax,2nd
1-4	Stp R 2nd,Dbl OST L NTO,	relax,in,Dwn
4-12	repeat L last 8 Cts	
12-16	Drop to floor R,P NTO L	R up limp wrist

It's Show Time / 160

Routines - More - Continued

COUNTS	BODY MOVEMENTS	ARMS
1-8	R heel Tp 2x Stp,JPDB face side 6 or side 8,chug Frt or Bck Cts 5,6,7 release Hd Bck,Sh Bck Pelv release Bck	2nd spiral,Dwn,relax
1-8	Repeat,face opposite sides	
1-8	Flex R Ft Cr,point R Ft 2nd,JPDB repeat L	Flex 2nd,stretch Cr,Dwn
1-16	Trp with flicks 8x,travel to new places on stage	limp wrist same flicks
1-8	Flex R Ft Cr,point R Ft 2nd,JPDB repeat L	flex 2nd,stretch Cr Dwn
1-8	2x Stp BC Frwd,high energy,4 Cuban Wks	Dwn 2x,scoop & press Dwn 2nd
1-8	Tp R,P R NTO 2x,Tp 2x R JPDB Trn L	R Sh up-Dwn 2x,relax,R Cr body L Hnd up,V,relax
1-8	Rond de jambe J Wks Frwd 4x	R wrap,L, V
1-8	Low J Wks to corner 4 3x,Trn R face Frt,face corner 2	L Hnd flick cts 1,3,5,7
1-8	Travel corner 2,Flap 3x,BC R-L,R flap BC,L flap BC,flap R,L,Stp	Dwn,flex
1-4	Stand croisé,Cont	scoop Frt Cts 1-3,rotate palms Twd face
5-8	Slow 2-St Trn L,P R NTO Tp R 2nd	Dwn,R flex in-out
ADAGIO SECTION		
	This section has only words, no music	
1-64	Slow movement of your choice	
PART 5		
1-8	Repeat 1st 8 Cts of PART 2	
1-8	Repeat 3rd 8 Cts of PART 2, pose of your choice on Ct 8	

End

Routines - Continued

▲ A Lyrical Adage

SOONER OR LATER
CHOREOGRAPHY: Marcus R. Alford
MUSIC: Song "Sooner or Later" from the album "Breathless" by Madonna
LEVEL: Intermediate-Advanced Jazz
Lyrical

* Costume suggested: skirt

COUNTS	BODY MOVEMENTS	ARMS
1-16	Wk on stage bluesey	
PART 1		
1-8	R Ft Bck,Stp R Tp L Ft Bck,look R Hnd	R curve up,L curve up,R Sh roll Bck,L Sh roll Bck,Sham R,L,R,L Hnd Bck Hd,R 2nd
1-8	L coupé Dev low croisé,Rond de jambe 2nd,JPDB,repeat R,with JPDB Trn R	Dwn relax,flowing shs
1-8	Stp L 2nd IS Cpt,Stp R,L,Dbl OST R, Plié Stp R 2nd P TO R,Rel L,lean L	L round,L up,Dwn,round drop,wrap R Frt,L Bck
1-8	Stp R,Horse Shoe R,P TO L,face corner 4	R Dwn L up,5th,R Cr Bck "L"
1-8	Batt BLO L Leg Frt,Stp L Batt R straight leg,Fouetté corner 2 to Arabq,Stp R,L	drop R Dwn,L Frwd,round, 1st Arabq high,drop
1-8	P R NTO Hp lift,roll Hps 2x L,arch BLO little weight on L Ft,look up to Ct 8	Dwn,V,L Hnd R wrist,Dwn body slowly
1-8	Piqué with L Ft 3x corner 1,St L Ct 7 Tp R Ft NTO Ct 8	LJA,Bck L Dwn,Sham R,LJA Bck R,drop R
1-8	corner 4,Stp R,L,R,IS Cpt end corner 3 L leg IS Cpt face Frwd	drop,round R up,Repeat L
1-8	Stp R,L,R IS Cpt,Stp L,drape R Ft TI to L leg	R round,R up,R,L,Hps, elbows out
PART 2		
1-8	Tp R,Stp R,JPDB Trn L,Cr R over L, Horse shoe Trn R	Hnd R Hp,V,Dwn,wrap R Frt R up,L Dwn
1-8	P R TO,Dev R corner 2 Plié Rel L,Stp R,L,coupé R hold Cts 6-8,look corner 2 Ct 8	Dwn,2nd spiral,L Sh up
1-8	Stp R SLO L leg up,1-4,P NTO L,Trp Bck 7&8	R Dwn L up,look R,R up, look R hnd Dwn
1-8	Face Bck,Stp L IS Rond de jambe,St R,L,Repeat L	spiral & Press R,L

Routines - Sooner or Later - Continued

COUNTS	BODY MOVEMENTS	ARMS
1-8	Stp L IS Rond de jambe,St R,L to Frt St IS Arabq Trn,IS NTO Trn Stp L Ct 8	spiral & Press R,round R,R up,round,Dwn
1-8	St R hop TO,L P Bck fall roll,end L Arabq on R knee(full Bck arch)	fist,JH,floor
1-4	Pose of your choice on floor	
5-8	R Swat look Bck over L Sh,reach L Frwd to Aud,R on floor look Frwd	
1-8	Stand slowly L Ft free	
1-48	Repeat L all of PART 1,(6 Cts of 8), Begin with L Ft,Pose of your choice on floor.	

End

Routines - Continued

▲ A Blues - Street Style Combination

FEVER
CHOREOGRAPHY: Marcus R. Alford
MUSIC: "Fever" by Chaka Khan (Original recording by Peggy Lee) song "Fever"
LEVEL: Intermediate-Advanced Jazz

COUNTS	BODY MOVEMENTS	ARMS
1-8	4 Wk R,L,R,L,2 Pvt face corner #1	JH R,L
1-8	Repeat	
1-8	Kck BC low 4th Pos Rel,St R St L leap R	JH R up,L Hp. 2nd Arabq
1-16	Trp R St L BLO R To floor,Dev L up,cr L over R split L out,sit spin L,stand up 2nd Pos hold	2nd Pos,JH R up
1-8	P R,L,R Tp R Rel 5th,St I Tp R (Hd shake 1 &a2)	R JWP,L Hp,JWP Bow&Arrow,JWP R
1-8	St R IS Cpt brush R cr L BLO	R in,diag R JH 2nd
1-4	P R TI St R	scoop up press
1-8	St L St R OST Trn(s),JPDB Trn L St R St L	

PART 2

COUNTS	BODY MOVEMENTS	ARMS
1-8	Tp St R Tp St L,4 wks in place, R,L,R,L	reach R JH,fists to Hps,2x,R fist up-Dwn,up-Dbl Dwn
1-8	Repeat above St	
1-8	St Bck R Tp L,St side L Tp R, smmy L,Hd Bck ct 8	snap R,R across Collar Bone,smmy R Hnd
1-8	TO R slowly,accent ct 4,Hd BckR ct 5,look corner 1 ct 6,look Frwd ct 7	JH slow across, accent ct.4
1-8	Batt R cr Tp L,St L cr cabriole, St R St L grab knee	L "L" high 1st L
1-8	Dev R leg St R,look Bck corner 2	R calf,sham L,R wrap,Hnds on Bck
1-8	Wk R,L,R,L,TI R P R TI Plié Rel L	shake R finger, snap R up, V up
1-4	cr R over L slow soutenu Trn	clap Hnds Frt,JH Bck Hd
1-8	2nd Pos small Jumps,accent cts	Bck Hd, V & drop 2,4,6,8, 4x

Routines - Fever - Continued

COUNTS	BODY MOVEMENTS	ARMS

PART 3

1-8	lie on R side, Dev L up	5th
1-8	Plié L ft with flex,split L Swat L lift Bck	
1-8	sit spin L, Look ct 5 hold ct 6, Dev R	
1-8	4 crab Wks Frwd, face side 5, begin R	
1-8	Bck roll on floor to kneel	JH R ct 5,R fist to R Hp ct 7,JH R ct 8
1-8	stay kneel	R Hnd L Sh,L Hnd R Sh roll Hd R,release to sit
1-4	Pose	
1-8	stand up to face Frt	Hnds on Hps
1-8	(ROUND) R leg over L,Trn face Bck,2x end to face Frt	JH R,L Hp 2x

(SOLO BREAKS) 8 counts of 8 and a 4

PART 4

1-8	St R Tp L St L Tp R,lazy Rond de jambe, 2x	Sq, JH Dwn, (Funky) R Hnd Rond de jambe
1-8	JPDB R OST Att L,P Tl L hitch Kck Hnd stand, Hd release	2nd Pos, fist on Hps JH 5th
1-8	(FLOOR WORK) open Swat R, Tl R,look at Aud ct 7	
1-8	stretch over R,R leg swing to L knee,swing R leg Bck Swat face corner 1	L Hnd R ft, R Hnd R knee
1-8	sit spin L face corner 4,look Frt ct 5, hold ct 6,7,8	R Hnd R knee
1-8	grande pas de cheval 2x,P Tl L Att look ct 7, corner 8L ankle	R Hnd R Knee, L Hnd
1-8	reach L arm up & over to side 5 ct 4, body collapse. Look side 5 on ct 5, look Frwd on ct 6,hold cts 7&8.	

End

NOTES

CHAPTER 6

WHERE DID JAZZ COME FROM?

Jazz is the style of music that seemed to originate in the southern part of the United States, especially New Orleans, late in the nineteenth century. There have been many changes in jazz which have resulted in many different styles however, there are certain elements common to all of them including improvisation, rhythm sections in ensembles, reliance on popular song form, and performer rather than composer orientation.

In trying to establish the origins of the word "jazz," it appears to have been first used in the *San Francisco Bulletin* on March 6, 1913.

> The team which speeded into town this morning comes pretty close to representing the pick of the army. Its members have trained on ragtime and 'jazz.'

On January 21, 1917, Damon Runyon wrote in his column for the Hearst papers,

> The Old Jaz Band
>
> New York. Jan 20. A Broadway cafe announces, as something new to the big Bright Aisle, the importations from the West of a syncopated riot known as a Jaz Band.

Walter Kingsley wrote in the New York Sun on August 5, 1917

> Whence comes jass?... Variously spelled Jas, Jass, Jaz, Jasz, and Jascz. The word is African in origin. It is common on the Gold Coast of Africa and in the hinterland of Cape Coast Castle....Jazz is based on the savage musician's wonderful gift for progressive retarding and acceleration guided by his sense of 'swing.'

The last decades of the 19th century saw the development of Jazz in America. Ragtime and Blues emerged together as the beginnings of jazz as we know it but the word "jazz" wasn't commonly used until around 1913. Where did the word itself originate? There are many theories: one suggests it was used as a minstrel or vaudeville term; another suggest Arabic or African origins; still another offers the explanation that "jazz" was possibly a synonym for the sex act; another possibility is that it is derived from the French word "jaser" which means "to chatter or have animated conversation among diverse people."

Alan P. Merriam and Fradley H. Garner, "Jazz-The Word."
Frank Tirro, *Jazz: A History*, pp. 51-56.

In the following section I have listed music by type and style to enable you to easily select music for your class or performance. Some artists are very versatile and will appear on more than one list.

There are many more artistis than I have mentioned in each category, however I have selected these as guidelines to help you choose appropriate music.

Music / 168

CLASSICAL JAZZ

Out Of The Blue
Widespread Jazz Orchestra
Sadao Watanabe

Alto Sax
Ornette Coleman
Hank Crawford
Johnny Hodges
Art Pepper
Phil Woods (& clarinet)
Benny Carter (& trumpet)

Bass
Ray Brown
Charles Mingus
Charnett Moffet

Big Band
Woody Herman

Clarinet/Dixieland Jazz
Pete Fountain

Congas/Bongos/Latin Jazz
Mongo Santamaria

Drums
Louie Bellson
Art Blakey
Jack DeJohnette
Elvin Jones
Gene Krupa
Shelly Manne
Buddy Rich (& orchestra)
Max Roach

Flute
Claude Bolling
Paul Horn
Herbie Mann

Guitar
George Benson
Kenny Burrell
Barney Kessel
Wes Montgomery
Joe Pass
John Scofield

New Orleans Jazz
Dirty Dozen Brass Band

Orchestra Toshiko Akiyoshi
Count Basie
Mercer Ellington
Heath Brothers

Orchestra/Big Band
Cab Calloway
Artie Shaw

Orchestra/Quartet
Dave Brubeck

Organ/Piano
Charles Earland
Jimmy McGriff

Piano
Chick Corea
Bill Evans
Gil Evans
Ahmad Jamal
Keith Jarret
Hank Jones
Scott Joplin
Steve Kuhn
Thelonious Monk
Jelly Roll Morton
Oscar Peterson
Andre Previn
George Shearing
Billy Strayhorn
Art Tatum
McCoy Tyler

Piano/Big Band/Orchestra
Stan Kenton

Piano/Orchestra
Erroll Garner
Earl 'Fatha' Hines

Piano/Organ
Dick Hyman

Piano/Ragtime
Fats Waller

Piano/Synthesizer/Orchestra
SunRa

Piano/Synthesizer
Herbie Hancock

Piano/Vocals
Harry Connick, Jr.
Dr. John

Ragtime
Eubie Blake

Sax
Cannonball Adderley
Gato Barbieri
Richie Cole
Dexter Gordon
Scott Hamilton
John Handy
Eddie Harris
Oliver Lake
Bradford Marsalis
Gerry Mulligan
Charlie Parker
Paul Winter

Sax/Clarinet
Chico Freeman

Music - Classical Jazz - Continued

Sax/Flute
James Moody

Soprano Sax/Flute
Joe Ferrell

Tenor Sax
Courtney Pine
John Coltrane
Eddie Daniels
Eddie 'Lockjaw' Davis
Johnny Griffin
Coleman Hawkins
Illinois Jacquet
Sandy Rollins
Pharaoh Sanders
Wayne Shorter
Stanley Turrentine
Zoot Sims

Tenor Sax/Flute
Lew Tabackin

Tenor Sax/Orchestra
Stan Getz

Trumpet
Chet Baker
Miles Davis
Dizzy Gillespie
Wynton Marsalis
Clark Terry

Trumpet/Dixieland Jazz
Al Hirt

Trumpet/FluegalHorn
Art Farmer
Freddie Hubbard

Trumpet/Orchestra/Vocals
Louis Armstrong

Trumpet/Orchestra
Maynard Ferguson
Quincy Jones
Doc Severinson

Vibes
Lionel Hampton
Bobby Hutcherson
Milt Jackson
Cal Tjader

Vibes/Piano
Gary Burton
Donal Byrd

Violin
Stephane Grappelli
Joe Venuti

Vocals
Billie Holiday
Mose Allison
Ernestine Anderson
Fred Astaire
Betty Carter
Billy Eckstine
Ella Fitzgerald
Lena Horne
Alberta Hunter
Cleo Laine
Carmen McRae
Lambert, Hendricks Ross
Flora Purim
Mel Torme
Sarah Vaughn
Dinah Washington
Joe Williams

Vocals/Piano
Nina Simone

BIG BANDS, COMPOSERS, AND SINGERS

David Amram
Louis Armstrong
Chet Baker
Charlie Barnet
Count Basie Orchestra
Sidney Bechet
Bix Beiderbicke
Louis Bellson
Irving Berlin
Black Eagle Jazz Band
Art Blakey
Ruby Braff and his "Allstars"
Clifford Brown
Les Brown and his Band of Renown
Ray Brown
Dave Brubeck
The Dave Brubeck Quartet
Gary Burton
Charlie Byrd
Benny Carter
Ray Charles
Buddy Childers Big Band
Judy Christy
Buck Clayton
Rosemary Clooney
Al Cohn
Ornette Coleman
John Coletrane
Eddie Condon
Chris Conner
Chick Corea
Bob Crosby and his Bobcats
Miles Davis
Buddy DeFranco
The Dorsey Brothers Band
Jimmy Dorsey and his Orchestra
Tommy Dorsey and his Orchestra
Dukes of Dixieland
Harry "Sweets" Edison
Roy Eldridge
The Duke Ellington Orchestra
The Duke Ellington Orchestra with Mercer Ellington
Ziggy Elman & His Orchestra
Bill Evans
Tal Farlow
Art Farmer
Maynard Ferguson
The Maynard Ferguson Orchestra
Ella Fitzgerald
Erroll Garner
George Gershwin
Stan Getz
Terry Gibbs
Astrud Gilberto
Benny Goodman
Benny Goodman & His Orchestra
The Benny Goodman Quartet
Dexter Gordon
Stephane Grappelli
Glen Gray & the Casaloma Orchestra
Buddy Greco
Lionel Hampton
Herbie Hancock
Coleman Hawkins
Erskie Hawkins & his Orchestra
Woody Herman
Earl "Fatha" Hines
Billy Holiday
Dick Hyman
Jackie (Cain) & Roy (Krahl)
Harry James and his Orchestra
Keith Jarrett
Bunk Johnson
J.J. Johnson
Hank Jones
Quincy Jones
Hal Kemp & His Orchestra
Stan Kenton
Stan Kenton and his Orchestra
Barney Kessel
Morgana King
Rahsaan Roland Kirk
Lee Konitz
Gene Kruppa Big Band
Michel Legrand
George Lewis
Mel Lewis & the Jazz Orchestra
Abbey Lincoln
Howard McGhee

Music - Big Bands, Composers, and Singers - Continued

Dave McKenna
Marian McPartland
Chuck Mangione
Herbie Mann
Shelley Manne
Charlie Mariano
Branford Marsalis
Wynton Marsalis
Glenn Miller (Big Band)
Charles Mingus
The Modern Jazz Quartet
Miff Mole
Thelonius Monk
Russ Morgan
Gerry Mulligan
The New York Jazz Quartet
Red Nichols & His Five Pennies
Red Norvo
Charlie Parker
Art Pepper
Oscar Peterson
Bud Powell
Tito Puente and His Latin Ensembles
Boyd Raeburn & His Orchestra
Django Reinhardt
Buddy Rich
Max Roach
Shorty Rogers
Pee Wee Russell
Gunther Schuller
Bud Shank
Artie Shaw (Big Band)
Charlie Shavers

BLUES MUSIC

Blues Music, normally slower, generally has a theme or story line. Blues is strong and has excellent music breaks.

Bobby Blue Bland
Nappy Brown
Ruth Brown
Ray Charles
Albert Collins (Guitar, Vocals)
Ry Cooder (Guitar)
James Cotton
Rober Cray (Guitar, Vocals)
Willie Dixon
Aretha Franklin
Z.Z. Hill
John Lee Hooker (Keyboards)
Lightning Hopkins (Guitar, Keyboards)
Etta James
Albert King (Guitar)
B.B. King (Guitar, Vocals)
Freddie King
Alberta Hunter
Leadbelly
Little Milton
Ester Phillips
Professor Longhair (Piano)
Leon Redbone
Otis Rush
Bessie Smith
Taj Mahal
Koko Taylor
Rufus Thomas
Big Mama Thornton
Joe Turner
Ruby Turner
Bernie Wallace (Keyboards, Vocals)
Little Walter
Ethal Waters
Muddy Waters (Guitar, Vocals)
Kathie Webster
Jimmy Witherspoon
Howlin Wolf (Guitar, Vocals)

JAZZ ROCK FUSION

This music has a backbeat and normally maintains a steady, countable rhythm base.

Gerald Albright (Sax)
Roy Ayers (Keyboard)
Gato Barbieri (Sax)
Walter Beasley (Sax)
David Benoit (Piano)
Arthur Blythe (Sax)
George Benson (Guitar)
Angela Bofill (Vocal)
Brecker Brothers (Horns)
Alex Bugnon (Piano)
Donald Byrd (Trumpet)
Stanley Clark (Bass, Guitar)
Billy Cobham (Drums)
Nat King Cole (Vocal)
Michel Colombier (Keyboard)
Norman Connors (Producer)
Chick Corea (Keyboard,Composer)
Larry Coryell (Guitar)
Bing Crosby (Vocal)
PaQuito D'Riveria (Sax)
Eddie Daniels (Clarinet)
Miles Davis (Trumpet)
Deodato (Keyboard)
George Duke (Keyboard)
Richard Elliot (Sax)
Kevin Eubanks (Guitar, Fusion)
Wilton Felder (Bass)
Victor Feldman (Vibes)
Rodney Franklin (Piano)
Michael Franks (Vocal)
Cabo Frio (Jazz Fusion)
Kenny G (Sax)
Eric Gale (Guitar)
Judy Garland (Vocal)
Tom Grant (Piano)
Dave Grusin (Sax, Asst)
Jan Hammer (Keyboard)
Herbie Hancock (Keyboard, Asst)
John Handy (Sax)
Hiroshima
Paul Horn (Flute)
Bobbi Humphrey (Flute)

Bob James (Keyboard, Composer)
Al Jarreau (Vocal)
Quincy Jones
Stanley Jordan (Guitar)
John Klemmer (Sax)
Earl Klugh (Guitar)
Ladysmith Black Mambazo (Vocal, Acapella)
Hubert Laws (Flute)
Victor Lazlo (Vocal from Belgium)
Peggy Lee (Vocal)
Jeff Lorber (Fusion)
Ralph MacDonald (Percussion)
Chuck Mangione (Flugelhorn)
Gap Mangione (Piano)
The Manhattan Transfer (Vocals)
Herbie Mann (Flute)
Tania Maria (Piano, Vocal)
Hugh Masekela (Trumpet)
Harvey Mason (Trumpet)
David Matthews (Composer,Keyboards)
Marcus Miller (Bass, Guitar)
Rob Mullins
Les McCann (Piano)
Bobby McFerrin (Vocal)
Sergio Mendes (Orch)
Pat Methany (Guitar,Composer)
Rob Mounsey and the Flying Monkey Orchestra
Najee (Sax)
Oregon
Passport
Pieces of a Dream
Jean Luc Ponty (Violin)
Preservation Hall Band (Dixieland,Ragtime)
Tito Puente (Percussion,Latin Jazz)
Lou Rawls (Vocal)
Diane Reeves (Vocal)
Lee Ritenour (Guitar)
Patrice Rushen (Vocal)
Sade (Vocal)
Joe Sample (Piano)
Ester Satterfield (Vocal)
David Sanborn (Sax)

Music - Jazz Rock Fusion - Continued

Diane Schurr (Vocal)
Tom Scott (Sax)
Marlena Shaw (Vocal)
Wayne Shorter (Sax)
Frank Sinatra (Vocal)
Sky
Lonnie Liston Smith (Piano)
Spyro Gyra
Tuck and Patti (Guitar,Vocal)
Stanley Turrentine (Tenor sax)
Special EFX
Dave Valentin (Flute)
Bernie Wallace (Piano,Composer)
Grover Washington, Jr. (Sax)
Ernie Watts (Sax)
Weather Report
Tim Weisberg (Flute)
Kirk Whalum (Sax)
Lenny White (Keyboard)
Nancy Wilson (Vocal)
Yellow Jackets
Joe Zawinul (Piano,Keyboard)

NEW AGE JAZZ MUSIC

This music is usually melodic and has a recurring theme.

William Ackerman (Guitar)
Acoutic Alchemy
Suzanne Ciani
Enigma
ENYA
Michael Hedges (Guitar)
Michael Jones (Piano)
Kitaro
David Lanz and Paul Speer
Jean Michel Jarre
Ray Lynch
Mannheim Steamroller
Shadowfax
Liz Story (Piano)
Tangerine Dream
Vangelis
Andreas Vollenweider
George Winston (Piano)
Yanni

CONTEMPORARY/CURRENT JAZZ MUSIC

Even though this music dates itself, because of its fresh, new sound, it has a definite place in both the classroom and in performance routines. Some of the artists are established and are accepted by a wide audience while still others are very temporary.

Paula Abdul
Mustapha Addy (Afro)
Art of Noise
Patty Austin
Big Audio Dynamite
Anita Baker
B-52's
Harry Belafonte
George Benson
Matt Biano
Basia
Big Twist and the Mellow Fellows
   (Blues/Chicago Blues)
Blues Brother
Bobby Brown
James Brown
Jerry Butler
Buckwheat Zydeco
Chuck Berry
Willie Colon (Latin jazz)
Chicago
Joe Cocker
Natalie Cole
Sam Cooke
Kid Creole and the Coconuts (Latin style)
Earth, Wind, and Fire
Emerson, Lake, and Palmer
Eurythmics
Falco (German vocal)
Roberta Flack
Dan Fogelberg
Aretha Franklin
Marvin Gaye
Philip Glass
Al Green (includes Gospel)
Gypsy Kings (Spanish/Flamenco/Latin)
Donny Hathaway
Isaac Hayes
Nona Hendryx
Jennifer Holiday

Linda Hopkins
Geoge Howard (Soprano Sax)
Isley Brothers
Joe Jackson
Janet Jackson
Michael Jackson
Al Jarreau
Rick James
Jellybean (Producer/Vocal)
Elton John
Billy Joel
Grace Jones
Chaka Khan
Gladys Knight and the Pips
Patti Labelle
Vickor Lazlo
Little Richard
Lyle Lovett (Western-like/some Blues)
Paul McCartney
Bobby McFerrin
Bette Midler
Miami Sound Mchine (Latin-like)
Liza Minelli
Billy Ocean
The Pointer Sisters
Prince
Queen Ida and her Zydeco Band
Leon Redbone
Otis Redding
Linda Ronstadt
Diana Ross
Leon Russel
Sade
Rare Silk
Andrews Sisters
Soul II Soul
Steely Dan
Carly Simon
Phoebe Snow
Cat Stevens

Music - Contemporary/Current - Continued

Donna Summers
Talking Heads
Tramaine Hawkins (also Gospel)
Thompson Twins
Tina Turner/Luther Vandross
Gino Vannelli
Was Not Was
Tom Waits
World Saxophone Quartet
Stevie Wonder (also producer)
Yello

CONCLUSION

Jazz Danceology is an idea born of a need I recognized as I taught jazz across the country. Because jazz is such a new art form, knowledge and understanding are limited. Though there were many teachers in my classes who had had the opportunity to learn and understand the terminolgy and technique, there were many more who had not. Since technique is the framework on which jazz builds, before I could teach, I had to find a common ground... we had to "speak the same language" which meant that a portion of the very precious time we had together was spent covering terminology and basic technique. Before there can be individuality and self expression, before one can "break the rules," one must first know and understand them.

I was fortunate in my formative years to have been exposed to and guided by some of the true jazz greats. I was given the fundamentals and the structure from which I was able to see the essence of jazz. I was given a gift of learning which grows as it is shared. With *Jazz Danceology*, I am sharing my gift with you. I believe that Jazz embodies life. It is every feeling, every mood, every emotion. Its boundaries are limitless.

I have attempted to define jazz dancing as it is recognized today. The terminology and techniques are essential elements of any jazz class and the more you, as a teacher know, the more you will be able to grow...and more important, the more you will be able to give your students. Only then will jazz become a true American art form that will survive our dance world and extend into the future.

NOTES

Appendix

BALLET TERMS FREQUENTLY USED IN JAZZ DANCE

ADAGE (Adagio)- a slow controlled movement or motion
EN L'AIR- in the air
ALLEGRO- Lively, sprightly type of movement(s)
ARABESQUE- an Arabian design. A position in dance where the weight is placed on the supporting leg and the other leg is lifted behind. It is executed at various heights.
ASSEMBLÉ- to bring or join together
ATTITUDE- posture. A position in dance in which the leg is lifted and bent in various degrees and directions - front, side, or back.
EN AVANT- in the front.
BATTEMENT- to beat
BARRE- the place where exercises are executed...at the barre or center barre.
CABRIOLE- a caper, leap. One leg is beaten against the other while in the air.
CHANGEMENT- to change (usually applies to the activity of the feet/legs in a jump.)
CHASSÉ- to chase or slide after
CHAÎNÉ - a chain. A turn that is normally performed after another (step, step)
COUPÉ- to cut. The foot is lifted and placed around the ankle.
CROISÉ - Crossed. This refers to the position of the legs or body in relation to the audience. This is the opposite of effacé or ouvert (open).
DÉGAGÉ - to disengage from the floor. Normally speaking of the foot from a ballet (classical) position.
EN DEDANS- Inward motion as in turns and Rond de Jambe(s)
EN DEHORS- Outward motion (away from) as in turns and Rond de Jambe(s)
EN CROIX- a cross. In dance terms, an exercise that is performed front, side, back, side or vice versa.
DEMI- half
DEUX- two (as in Pas de Deux)
DEVANT- in front
DERRIÈRE- behind you
DÉVELOPPÉ - to unfold (develop) the leg. Also can refer to the arms.
ÉCHAPPÉ - to escape. The feet are open from one another
ENVELOPPÉ - to envelope or enfold.
FONDU- to melt. A movement executed standing on one leg. Bend supporting leg with the other leg lifted in varying degrees into coupé or passé.
FOUETTÉ whipped. In dance, where a leg goes through positions in the air. For example, battement forward, fouetté to arabesque.
GLISSADE- a sliding step
GRAND-big or large
JETÉ -to be thrown
OUVERT - open in relationship to the dancer's body or the audience.
PAS DE BOURRÉE- a movement in dance (classical ballet) where a series of steps, whether picked up or close to the floor is executed.
PAS DE CHEVAL - a step of the horse... a pawing motion of the foot or leg.
PAS DE CHAT- step of the cat. Passé to passé leap normally performed sideways ending in 4th or 5th.
PETIT- small

Appendix - Continued

PENCHÉ- to tilt (pitch) down or to one side. For example, penche arabesque
PIQUÉ - to prick..To step upon a straight leg. Step right on straight leg, left leg can be in 2nd or in attitude but more often is in passé.
PORT DE BRAS- carriage or movement of the arms
RELEVÉ- to rise up as high as possible on your toes
ROND DE JAMBE- the rounding of the leg
SAUTÉ - to jump
SISSONNE- a movement in which the weight is transferred from one foot to the other in a jumping motion...may be performed front, side or back.
TENDU- to stretch...usually speaking of an action of the foot
TOUR- to turn

Abbreviations For Terminology & Techniques

Arabq	Arabesque
Att	Attitude
Aud	Audience
Batt	Battement
BC	Ball change
Bck	Back (place back or face back of audience or stage)
BLO	Back Lay Out
BR	Bridge
Ch	Chassé (chase)
CHA	Chaîné (turn)
CCC	CHA-CHA-CHA
Cst	Charleston Step
Cg	Chug
Cpt	Compass turn
Cont	Contraction
Ct(s)	Count(s)
Cr	Cross
Dbl	Double
Dev	Développé
Diag	Diagonal
Dig	Dig
Dwn	Down
Dg	Drag
Ext	Extend or extension
Fn Kck	Fan Kick
FLO	Front Lay Out
Frwd	Forward
Frt	Front (face forward)
Ft	Foot
Fts	Feet
Gd	Grind
Gyr	Gyration
Hd	Head
Hnd(s)	Hand(s)
HitKck	Hitch Kick
Hp(s)	Hip(s)
IS	Inside
IST	Inside Turn
J	Jazz
JBug	Jitterbug (as in movement)
JPDB	Jazz Pas de Bourrée
JH	Jazz Hand
JWP	Jazz wrist press (also known as JRP)
Kck	Kick
L	Left
Ly	Lindy (as in a style of jitterbug-like movement.)

Appendix - Continued

LOD	....	Line of Direction (direction/focus of movement)
Lg	....	Lunge
NTO	....	No turn out
Opp	....	Opposite
OST	....	Outside turn
P	....	Passé
Pdt	....	Paddle turn (as in tap dance)
Par	....	Parallel
Pelv	....	Pelvis
Plié	....	Plié (to bend)
Plié Rel	....	Plié Relevé
Pvt	....	Pivot
Pos	....	Position
1st	....	first position
2nd	....	second position
3rd	....	third position
4th	....	fourth position
5th	....	fifth position
R	....	Right
RC	....	Rib Cage
Rel	....	Relevé
Sham	....	Shampoo
Sh(s)	....	Shoulder(s)
Sk	....	Shake
Sl	....	Slide
SLO	....	Side Lay Out
Smmy	....	Shimmy
SOF	....	Sitting on Floor
Splt	....	Split
Sq	....	Square
Srt	....	Strut
St	....	Step
Stp	....	Stomp
Sut	....	Soutenu Turn
Sug Ft	....	Sugar Foot
Swat	....	Swaztika
Tm	....	Tempo (as in reference to timing)
Tp	....	Tap (as in foot action)
TO	....	Turn Out
TI	....	Turn In
Trn	....	Turn
Trp	....	Jazz Triplet
TT	....	Table Top
Twd	....	Toward
X's	....	Number of times something is performed (repetitions)
V	....	"V" position (arms and/or legs)
Wg	....	Wiggle
Wk(s)	....	Walk(s)

BIBLIOGRAPHY

Berkson, Robert. *Musical Threater Choreography.* New York: Back Stage Books, 1990.

Blum, Lynn Anne and Chaplin, L. Tarim. *The Intimate Act of Choreography.* Pittsburgh: University of Pittsburgh Press, 1982.

Clark, Mary and Crisp Clement. *History of Dance.* New York: Crown Publishers, 1981.

Feather, Leon. *The Encyclopedia of Jazz.* New York: DaCapo Press, Inc., Horizon Press, 1960.

Giordano, Gus. *American Jazz Dance* Printed and under the auspices of the National Council of Dancer Teacher Organization, Inc., 1966.

Giordano, Gus. *Anthology of American Jazz Dance.* Illinois: Orion Publishing, 1978.

Grant, Gail. *Technical Manual and Dictionary of Classical Ballet.* New York: Dover Publications, Inc., 1982.

Humphrey, Doris. *The Art of Making Dances.* New York: Grove Press, Inc., 1959.

Jump Into Jazz. California: Mayfield Publishing Company, 1990. (Second Edition)

Mackie, Joyce. *Basic Ballet - 7 Steps Defined.* New York: Viking Penquin, Inc., 1978.

Pica, Rae. *Dance Training for Gymnastics.* Illinois: Leisure Press, 1988.

Stearns, Marshall and Stearns, Jean. *Jazz Dance: The Story of American Vernacular Dance.* New York. Schirmer Books, 1968.

Sutton, Tommy. *Tap Along With Tommy* 1986.

Terry, Walter, Jr. *The Dance in America.* New York: Harper & Row, 1956, 1971

Thorpe, Edward. *Black Dance.* New York: Overlook Press, 1989.

Tirro Frank. *Jazz: A History.* New York: W.W. Norton & Co., 1977.

Traguth, Fred. *Modern Jazz Dance.* (Volumes 1 and 2). Wilhelmshaven, West Germany: Florian Noetzel, 1983.

Index

A
Adult Jazz Class, 137
Advanced Jazz Class, 136
Afro-Jazz, 41
Airplane, 57
Assemblé, 102, 104
Asymmetrical Combinations, 136
Attitude Turn, 112
Attitude, Turned In, 101

B
Back - Shoulders, 71
Back Layout, 85
Balance, 111
Ballet Terms, 181, 182
Barre, 46
Barrel Turn, 47, 112
Baseball Bat, 57
Bassing, Judy Ann, 13
Bennett, Michael, 11
Bentz, Douglas, 14
Bethel, Pepsi, 13
Bezuglaya, Tatina, 14
Bezugly, Sergie, 14
Big Bands/Composers/Singers, 171, 172
Blues, 37
Blues Music, 173
Body Roll, 48, 135
Bow and Arrow, 57
Bridge, 49, 50, 51, 134
Broadway/Theatrical, 38
Butterfly, 56

C
Calypso, 42
Camel Walk, 77
Canon, 140
Carlos, Ernest, 31
Center Barre, 46, 131
Cha-Cha-Cha, 77, 78
Chaîne Turn, 112
Chassé, 78, 102
Chest Lift, 52
Children's Jazz Class, 137
Choreography, Successful, 139, 140
Chug, 52
Classical Jazz, 169, 170
Classroom Diagrams, 141, 142, 143
Cole, Jack, 10
Comb, 58
Compass Turn, 52, 102, 113

Contemporary/Current Jazz Music, 177, 178
Contract, 53, 64, 69, 135
Cool Jazz, 39
Coordination Exercises, 134
Corkscrew Turn, 113
Crab Walk, 53
Cross, Keith Anthony R., 15
Crossed Swastika, 98, 102
Cuban, 77, 79

D
D'Amore, Vic, 15
Darwin, Lea, 16
Day, Annie, 16
De Mille, Agnes, 10
DeMarco, Ronnie, 17
Développé Leap, 108
Diagonal Pulse, 69
Double Attitude, 109
Double Attitude Grand Jeté, 104
Double Attitude Jump/Leap, 53
Double Time, 53
Dr. Feelgood, 152, 153
Drape, 58
Dunham, Katherine, 10

E
Ellington, Mercedes, 17
Everybody Dance, 149, 150, 151
Exercises - Second Position, 125
Exercises - Standing, 125, 132
Exercises - Standing/Floor/Standing, 120, 121, 122, 123, 124

F
Fan Kick, 54, 102
Fever, 164, 165
Finger Fan, 59
First Arabesque Turn, 114
Fist, 59
Flat Back, 55
Flea Hop/Slide, 56, 102
Flick, 56
Flick Kick, 95
Floor Exercises, 132
Floor Stretch, 125
Floor Work, 46, 134
Fosse, Bob, 11
Frances-Fischer, Jana, 9
Frog, 56, 134
Frog Jump, 104
Front - Shoulders, 71

Front Layout, 86

G
Giacobbe, Joseph, 18
Giordano, Gus, 8, 11, 18
Gold, Sherry, 19
Goose Neck, 64
Grand Jeté, 108
Grand Jeté Leap Turn, 104
Grand Pas De Cheval, 109
Grand Rond De Jambe, 109
Grapevine, 80, 102
Grubb, Lynette, 19

H
Half Time, 56
Hatchett, Frank, 20
Hendry, Ginny East, 21
Hess, Cathy Lee, 21
High/Vegas, 81
Hip Lift, 67
Hitch Kick, 105
Horseshoe, 57, 102
Hot Jazz, 38
Hurdlers' Leap, 106
Hyperextension, 129, 134

I
Injuries, Prevention of, 44
Inside Turn, 114
Intermediate Jazz Class, 135
Isolation - Hands and Arms, 57
Isolation - Head, 64
Isolation - Hips, 67
Isolation - Rib Cage, 69
Isolation - Shoulders, 71
Isolations, 57
Ivey, Robert, 22

J
Jack Knife, 73
Jazz Dancing, History of, 9, 31
Jazz Hands, 59, 60, 77
Jazz Pas de Bourrée, 74, 81, 102
Jazz Pas de Bourrée Turn, 115
Jazz Rock Fusion, 174, 175
Jazz Runs, 77
Jazz Split, 75, 102
Jazz Square, 76, 81, 102
Jazz Triplet, 81, 100
Jazz Walks, 77
Jazz Wrist Press, 60
Jazz, Origin of, 10, 167, 168

Appendix / 186

K

Kelly, Charles, 22
Kimbo, 81
Kingsley, Walter, 168
Kisner, Meribeth, 23
Knee Hinge, 85
Kossman, Dagmar, 23
Kossover, Herb, 24
Kruse, T. Meriah, 24

L

L, 60
Large Patterns, 131
Latin, 41, 78, 79
Layouts, 85
Lindy, 87
Locomotive Movements, 87, 134
Long Jazz Arm, 61
Low Jazz Run, 82
Low Jazz Walk, 82
Luigi, 11, 25
Lyrical, 37

M

Mambo, 78
Mattox, Matt, 11, 25
Mazo, Joseph H., 5
Minimum Age for Jazz, 133
Modern Jazz, 39
More, 159, 160, 161
Morrison, Charlie, 31

N

Neutral, 87
New Age Jazz Music, 176
Noble, Duncan, 26
Notation, 144

O

Obey, Pattie, 26
Oklahoma, 10
Olmedo, Amparo, 27
Outside Turn, 116

P

Paddle Turn, 116
Partner Stretches, 127, 128, 129, 130
Pas de Chat, 47
Passé Neutral Hip Lift, 67, 88
Passé Turn, 117
PBS Theory, 111
Pencil Turn, 116
Perch, 88
Pike Jump, 106
Pivot, 89, 102
Placement, 44, 111, 126
Placement Studies, 132

Plié, 90, 91, 102
Plié - 1st Position, 90
Plié - 2nd Position, 90
Plié - 3rd Position, 91
Plié - 4th Position, 91
Plié - 5th Position, 91
Plié Relevé, 90, 91, 92, 102
Plow, 92
Plumb Line, 44, 45
Powlus, Peter, 27
Prance, 106
Pre-jazz, 133
Preparations, 83, 102
Primus, Pearl, 10
Profile, 64

R

Rebel, Gunther, 28
Red Hot Chicago, 147, 148
Release, 65, 68, 69, 92
Rib Cage Roll, 70
Rib Cage Side, 70
Rib Cage Square, 70
Robbins, Jerome, 10, 31
Robinson, Bill "Bojangles", 10
Rock, 40
Roll, 65, 68, 71
Roll Up, 93
Runyon, Damon, 168
Russian Jump, 93, 108

S

S Curve, 61
Saut de Chat, 108
Schulte-Kölpin, Petra, 28
Scoop, 61
Scoop and Press, 94
Second Position - Arms, 61
Second Position Hop, 107
Second Position Jump, 108
Second Position Leap, 108
Shampoo, 62, 77, 113
Sheer, Vickie, 29
Shimmy, 72
Shoulder Stand, 95
Side Layout, 86
Side to Side, 66, 68
Siegenfield, Billy, 29
Sissonne, 108
Slice, 62
Snap Kick, 95
Sooner or Later, 162, 163
Soutenu Turn, 117
Spencer, Bill, 30
Spider, 82
Spiral, 83, 96
Split, 75, 135
Split Leap, 108

Spotting, 111
Square, 96
Stag, 96, 109
Stage Diagrams, 141, 142, 143
Staging, 140
Step Ball Change, 83, 102
Stewart, Delia, 30
Stone, Art, 31
Strut, 84
Styles of Jazz Dance, 37
Sugar Foot, 97
Sutton, Tommy, 31
Swastika, 97, 102
Swing, 66
Switch Leap, 98, 109
Swivel, 68
Symmetrical Combinations, 135

T

Table Top, 55, 98, 99
Tap Step Turn, 117
Teen Jazz Class, 137
Temp de Fleche, 105
Terminology & Technique
 Abbreviations, 145, 146, 183, 184
Three Step Turn, 118
Tilt, 66
Traguth, Fred, 32
Trance Dance, 157, 158
Tremaine, Joe, 32
Triplet, 100, 102
Tuck Jump, 109

U

Up and Over, 92
Up/Down - Shoulders, 72

V

V Position, 63, 101

W

War Dance, 154, 155, 156
Warm Up, 134
West Coast, 40, 62, 84
West Side Story, 10, 31, 78, 82
Windmill, 63
Wrist Roll, 63

Y

Youmans, Dan, 33